D1474929

CAESAREAN MOON BIRTHS

CAESAREAN MOON BIRTHS

Calculations, Moon Sighting, and the Prophetic Way

HAMZA YUSUF

ZAYTUNA INSTITUTE

Published by Zaytuna Institute, 2007

Editor: Safir Ahmed
Managing Editor: Uzma Fatima Husaini
Copy Editor: Valerie Turner
Cover and Text Design: Abdallateef Whiteman
Cover Photograph: Youssef Ismail

ZAYTUNA INSTITUTE
2070 Allston Way, Berkeley, CA 94704
www.zaytuna.org
publications@zaytuna.org

ISBN: 978-0-9702843-2-7

Printed in the United States of America

بسم الله الرحمن الرحيم

IN THE NAME OF GOD, THE BENEFICENT, THE MERCIFUL

Prayers and blessings be upon the best of creation, our master Muḥammad, and upon his family and companions, and all who follow in their footsteps. Glory to the One who made the stars as guides for humanity and placed the sun and moon in exact courses to provide a means to measure time and learn calculation.

The Qur'an is the last prophetic dispensation revealed by God for humanity. Its guidance will remain until the Last Day, and no other infallible guidance will be given to the world until the return of the blessed prophet of God, Jesus, the Christ, who will affirm the Qur'an and elucidate its meanings conclusively for the community of our beloved Prophet ﷺ.

يَسْئَلُونَكَ عَنِ الأَهِلَّةِ قُلْ هِىَ مَوَقِيتُ لِلنَّاسِ والحَجِّ

They ask you about the crescent moons; say they are a means to measure your specific times and are also for the commencement of the hajj.

QUR'AN 2:189

صُوموا لِرؤْيَتِه وأفطِروا لرُؤيته ، فإن غُبِّيَ عليكم

فأكملوا عدَّة شَعبانَ ثلاثين

"Fast upon sighting [the new moon], and break the fast upon sighting it, and should it be obscured, then complete thirty days of Sha'bān."

A SAYING OF THE PROPHET MUḤAMMAD ﷺ

CONTENTS

PREFACE

ALL RELIGIONS HAVE rites that connect people to sacred time and place. Indeed, devotional observances are the hallmark of religion and maintain its perpetuity. Islam is noted for sacred rites that are largely time-based but also include rites involving places. The central daily rite is prayer; the central weekly rite is congregation; the central monthly rite is monitoring the new moon; the central yearly rite is Ramadan; and the central rite of one's lifetime is pilgrimage to the House of God.

The Abrahamic religions are rooted in the mystery of time; sacred timekeeping is central to Judaism, Christianity, and Islam. The original Abrahamic way was entirely lunar. The Jewish ritual experience was centered around the lunar months. As time passed, the Jewish community moved from a lunar to a solar-lunar calendar. The Christians, who emerged out of Jewish tradition, abandoned the Jewish lunar calendar for a Roman solar one. Islam, uniquely, has maintained this ancient tie solely to the celestial phenomenon of the lunar month.

Prior to the advent of electricity, every night held the possibility of a celestial light show. People in even the most urban environments were exposed to the awe and majesty of the heavens, which clearly "proclaim the glory of God."

The contemplation of the celestial orbs and their movements provided early man with the most direct connection to his Lord. In the Qur'anic story of Abraham, it is his observance of heavenly phenomena that leads him to his certainty of God's unity and transcendence. Since the time of the Seljuq Turks, the crescent moon has been a sign of Islam. Today, for instance, it serves in place of the cross for the relief work of the Muslim medics of the Red Crescent in Muslim lands.

Of late, certain Muslims, responding to the yearly anarchy in determining the beginning of Ramadan, have called for a move to calculations and an abandonment of the traditional practice of physical observation to determine the new moon. Some highly qualified mathematicians and astronomers believe that Muslims in North America should follow lunar months determined by calculation. They argue that the science of astronomy is highly developed and visibility charts can be generated to high degrees of precision; that calculation will help the Muslim community gain recognition from the government for Muslim holidays, which would obviously need to be known in the previous year when calendars are prepared; that it is not against the Sunnah, as some scholars of the earliest period have accepted calculations as have others of the later period; and that many modern scholars are inclining toward this position in larger numbers.

As the argument has been presented, the call is buttressed by early Muslim opinions, isolated but authoritative nonetheless, which allowed calculation. I have written this essay to reveal what I believe to be the fallacies in that claim. As I substantiate in this paper, the few scholars who did permit calculation did so for only the 29th night, and then only if clouds or other atmospheric conditions obscured the twilight sky. I do not believe there is any evidence to support an argument for calculation unless it is based upon the early Fatimid position that the new moon begins with the separation of the sun and moon's monthly conjunction—an opinion rejected by consensus among Sunni scholars and almost all of the Shia scholars. A few late Muslim scholars of the nineteenth century, not mentioned in any of the papers I read, did acknowledge the advancement of astronomy and the reliability of calculation. Their colleagues, however, ignored their opinions.

Hence we find that before this modern period, authoritative Imams did not advocate the abandonment of a prophetic practice that has been continually applied throughout Muslim history and remains viable today. Oddly, the one argument that might have merit is not put forward by the current proponents of calculation: that is a *maqāṣadī* argument, i.e., one that looks at the aims and purposes of the sacred law. While I recognize that such an argument would seem reasonable given the relative hardships people in North America face in adjusting fixed secular schedules with fluid sacred ones each year, the presence of a clear and unambiguous text from the sound hadith makes *ijtihād* untenable. Indeed, it could even be argued that connecting people with the natural phenomenon in our selves and on the horizon—which is where we must look every month for the new moon—is a central aim and purpose of the religion itself.

Having said that, I do see a compromise possible between the two positions if the proponents of calculation would alter their sighting calculation criterion to a 12-degree angular separation instead of their current 9-degree separation, which allows for probable sighting only under perfect conditions. For several years now, in monthly crescent observations, we have found that the moon sighting visibility charts based upon a 12-degree separation in North America consistently concur with our physical sightings on the West Coast of the United States.

The current crisis is largely the result of the lack of a unified religious authority and the split in the scholarly community over local sightings as opposed to one global sighting for all Muslims. And while both positions are sound and have their proofs from the early Muslim community and are recognized by all of our juristic schools, the latter position is hard to adhere to, given what we know about the earth and its vastness and the fact that while the moon is born in one region it has yet to be in others. Despite that, we should not make the local/global issue a point of dissention or division in our communities. It would foster unity if we adhered to one moon sighting that is seen by sound witnesses anywhere in North America. Devotional practices based upon moon calculations will always split the community. Those who question why we cannot calculate our moon dates when we calculate our prayer times will find unequivocal answers in this paper.

My hope is that this book will alleviate confusion and provide clarity—and guidance for those who are fed up with the inability of our community to agree on matters of the utmost importance and who simply want to fast, and break the fast, without worrying that they are doing it at the wrong time. We can be unified on this issue if we develop trained moon-sighting committees throughout North America who are committed to going out every month and maintaining a religious duty. My intention is not to be divisive. My personal friendship and love for many of the people promoting calculation is not negotiable. They are scholars in their own right in their respective areas of expertise and I respect their scholarship and honor their friendship and fraternity. On this matter, however, I believe an egregious mistake has been made and my hope is that it can be redressed. May God grant us clarity in matters obscure and guidance in matters momentous.

HAMZA YUSUF
DANVILLE, CALIFORNIA
4 RAJAB 1428

بسم الله الرحمن الرحيم

CAESAREAN MOON BIRTHS[*]

INTRODUCTION

ALL OF THE acts of ritualized worship incumbent upon Muslims are related to time, and thus the measurement and the detailing of time's passage is a religious duty. According to ʿAbd al-Ḥayy al-Kattānī, maintaining time is a religious position to which the Prophet ﷺ himself appointed certain people in Medina. Islamic law considers sacred timekeeping (*tawqīt*) a communal obligation, so once someone in a community fulfills this duty, the rest of the community is relieved of it.[1] Not only is it a religious duty to monitor the sun and the moon's courses for prayer times and for the other acts of worship contingent upon certain months, but, according to the Prophet ﷺ, it is one of the most pleasing and beloved acts to God. The Prophet ﷺ said, "The most beloved of God's servants to God are those who monitor the sun and moon, engendering love of God in God's servants and love of God's servants in God." And in a sound narration

[*] The title "Caesarean Moon Births" was chosen for two reasons. Like a caesarean birth, the early announcements of the lunar months that have historically accompanied a calculated new moon are primarily the result of conforming to the scheduling requirements of modern bureaucratic societies. Also, it was the edict of Caesar that was instrumental in forcing the Jews to abandon their lunar calendar based on actual sighting and resorting to one based on calculations.

related by al-Ḥākim, the Prophet ﷺ said, "The best of God's servants are those who watch the sun, moon, stars, and shadows in order to remember God."[2]

In another hadith, the Prophet ﷺ said to Muʿādh before sending him to Yemen to act as a judge, "What will you base your judgments on?"

Muʿādh replied, "The Book of God."

The Prophet ﷺ then asked, "And should it not be in the Book of God?"

"Then the Sunnah of the Prophet," replied Muʿādh.

"And should you not find it in the Sunnah?" asked the Prophet ﷺ.

"Then I will exert my efforts completely and not falter."

To this, the Prophet ﷺ responded, "Praise is due to God, who has given the messenger of the Messenger of God success."

This hadith elucidates the methodology to be followed by any scholar attempting to understand an issue involving a legal ruling in the sacred law of Islam. There are four agreed upon sources of legislation:

1) The Qur'an, first and foremost, 2) the Sunnah, which comprises the words, deeds, and acknowledgments of the Prophet Muḥammad ﷺ, as transmitted through reliable sources, 3) the consensus of the Muslim scholars (*ijmaʿ*), and, finally, 4) analogical reasoning (*qiyās*) that is used as a last resort in the absence of definitive proofs. However, of these four, the two sources agreed upon for use as single sources are the Book of God and the Sunnah of the Prophet ﷺ. The Prophet ﷺ stated, "I have left you two things; as long as you hold to them, you will never stray: the Book of God and my Sunnah."

So the scholars first look to the Qur'an, then to the

Sunnah, and then to the consensus of the previous scholars, and then, finally, resort to independent reasoning (*ijtihād*). However, *ijtihād* is permissible only when there is no decisive and unequivocal text (*naṣṣ*) found in the Qur'an or the Sunnah; this is based upon the juristic principle, "There can be no *ijtihād* in light of an explicit text."

Another important axiom is that both the Qur'an and the Sunnah were revealed in Arabic, and any interpretation must be in accordance with the accepted linguistic meaning of those texts during the period of revelation, between 610 and 632 CE. It is proscribed to interpret the Qur'an in the Arabic of any other period. One may refer to authentic pre-Islamic poetry to determine the meanings of words because linguistic usages of that period were accepted at the time of the Qur'anic revelation. Immense human effort has been exerted in order to preserve the meanings of the Arabic language of the Prophet's time. No other religious community on earth has the level of certainty about their sacred scriptures' historical authenticity and lexical signification as Muslims do. This is due first to God's promise of scriptural preservation, and then to efforts of those scholars who codified the Qur'an and preserved the Arabic language in the voluminous lexicons of the first centuries of Islam.

THE PROBLEM

The lunar Islamic calendar follows the phases of the moon, beginning with the crescent moon and ending with the conjunction of the moon and the sun in their respective perceived movements around the earth. The time of one lunation or complete cycle of the moon is approximately 29.5 days. This must be averaged because the moon does not travel at a constant speed nor does it travel in a perfect circle but in an elliptical orbit around the earth. The moon's monthly cycle around the earth varies between 29.2 days and 29.8 days, which means that throughout the year there will be approximately six months in which there are twenty-nine days, and six months in which there are thirty days. The total number of days in a lunar year is approximately 354, which is eleven days shorter than the average solar year. In order to make the lunar years consistent with the solar, many pre-Islamic societies intercalated or added days to the lunar months. This enabled them to follow a lunar calendar without having it depart from the fixed seasons of the solar calendar. This was and remains the practice of the Jewish community, which intercalates a thirteenth month every three years in order to align the lunar and solar calendars. Interestingly, however, the Jews originally practiced a purely lunar calendar and introduced intercalation later. The pre-Islamic Arabs used a lunar calendar but both calculated and intercalated their calendars when suitable for their needs. Their general practice however was to rely on a physical sighting of the crescent moon.

The Islamic lunar calendar is not to be tampered with, as the Prophet ﷺ prohibited intercalation in his farewell address to his community during the final pilgrimage. Islam condemns intercalation, regarding it as a rejection of the natural order inherent in the perfection of the lunar calendar that God has provided humanity for measuring time. For this reason, in a number of hadith that have the status of infallible (*mutawātir*) and are thus on par with the legislative authority of any verse in the Qur'an, the Prophet ﷺ commanded Muslims to base their month on the physical sighting of the new moon and stipulated that if not seen on the twenty-ninth completed day of the previous month on a clear evening, or if clouds or other atmospheric barriers hinder visibility, then to complete thirty days and begin the new month on the following sunset, which would be on the thirty-first day following the previous sighting.

In the modern world, however, exact times are far more significant than they were in the premodern world because of the importance placed on mechanical clocks, trains, planes, and deadlines. For this reason, Saudi Arabian officials, who use the lunar calendar for all governmental activities, decided at a certain point to rely on calculation as a basis for their calendar in order to ensure that people use the same dates and that the dates can be predetermined to facilitate scheduling and other time concerns of a modern society. The criterion they use for calculation is the conjunction of an astronomical new moon occurring before sunset of the first day of their lunar calendar. Although convenient, this system can be as much as two days off an actual new crescent sighting. Errors, due to this fact, have occurred in the past.

Muslims in North America use a lunar calendar only for devotional purposes and have had recourse to various methods of determining the lunar months. The most prominent methods include local sighting, sighting anywhere in North America, a physical sighting anywhere globally, and calculated sighting. There is also the option of simply following Saudi Arabia, and some assert that since anyone wishing to make the pilgrimage must follow Saudi Arabia for the hajj determination, it logically follows to include Ramadan as well, especially since Saudi Arabia is the only country in the world that still uses a lunar calendar for its day-to-day scheduling. Another popular method is following family members who reside in Muslim countries, as the option of simply calling mom, dad, grandma, or grandpa overseas and going along with the dates of their calendar in Damascus, Cairo, Karachi, or elsewhere is emotionally comforting for some, especially when calling to wish "Eid mubārak" to family back home when they themselves are just getting up to finish the last day of fasting (since the family is in a time zone that is several hours ahead).

The essential problem, therefore, is that there are indeed various ways to start Ramadan in North America and each group puts forward its reasoning for a preferred method. Who then should we follow?

THE QUR'AN AND THE MOON

The Qur'an declares: *Surely the months with God are twelve in the book of God since the day He created the heavens and the earth; four of them are sacred* (9:36). Imam ᶜAbd Allāh b. Aḥmad al-Nasafī, the noted theologian and exegete, explains the meaning of this verse: "This verse is to clarify that the legal rulings in shariah are to be determined by lunar months that are calculated by the crescent moons irrespective of the solar calendar."[3] Thus, the Qur'an commands Muslims to use the lunar month for their devotional matters, but not necessarily their worldly affairs. Qadi Abū Bakr b. al-ᶜArabī cites the verse, *They ask you about the crescent moons; say they are a means to measure your specific times* (mawāqīt) *and are also for the commencement of the hajj* (2:189) and explains it thus:

> The wisdom in this is that God has made the sun and moon two of His signs, and it is related in some sources that He assigned to each an angel and decreed for them two points of rising. He moves them between the two [throughout the year] for two benefits: one worldly, which is the solar calendar, and the other religious, which is based upon the lunar.[4]

Since two major obligatory acts of devotion and many minor recommended ones have designated times throughout the year, the lunar months have been given to specify those times. The word used for "specific times" is *mawāqīt* and is derived from the Arabic word *waqt*, which means "time." The difference between the word *waqt* and the other Arabic word for time, *zamān*, is that "*zamān* is absolute time and [refers to] the movements of the celestial orbs that indicate it from their starting point to their finishing point. So *zamān* is the division of time into past, present, and future, whereas *waqt* is *zamān* when it specifies a point that is for some specific affair."[5] Thus, the crescent moons were designated for determining specific times within the flow of time.

An intriguing aspect of the verse mentioned above is that it was revealed in response to those who asked the Prophet ﷺ about the crescents, and they were seeking to understand the actual mechanism, that is, the *science* of the crescent. They wanted to know how the moon did what it was doing. However, the Qur'anic response enlightened them that more important than their question of how, is why. This is the essential difference between science and religion, and is summed up in this one momentous verse of the Qur'an. The verse immediately following God's reply to their question is, *Do not enter houses through their back doors.* Some commentators understood that to mean, "Ask the right question: why, not how."

Our English word "month" is derived from "moon." In fact, the earliest human calendars were lunar, and it was lunar calendars and the human need to determine time's progression, especially the passage of the year itself, that led to the development of mathematics. This purpose is clearly stated in the verse, *It is God who made the sun shine and the moon glow, and determined the lunar phases that you may know the number of years and calculation* (10:5). According to Ibn ʿAbbās and others, "That you may know the number of years and calculation (*ḥisāb*)," was interpreted to mean that the 28 divisions or mansions (*manāzil*) of the moon allowed man to calculate which phase of the month he was in, thus enabling him to measure his days, given that there are twenty-eight phases of the month determined by the lunar mansions and on the twenty-ninth the moon disappears for a day or two only to re-emerge as a newborn crescent. However, it also implies that the challenge of measuring time gave man an impetus to learn and develop mathematics, and by extension, science. Hence, the sun and the moon following clear courses enabled humanity to track them and in so doing, increase our knowledge of science.

In his book on the calendar, David Duncan writes, "A case can be made that science itself was first sparked by a human compulsion to comprehend the passing of time, to wrestle down the forward motion of life and impose on it some sense of order."[6] The Muslim contribution to mathematics is immense and is largely a result of Muslim scientists attempting to forecast the appearance of new moons, find the precise qibla, and determine inheritance portions accurately. Muslims further developed Greek plane trigonometry as well as spherical trigonometry; interestingly, they considered spherical trigonometry as a separate science from plane trigonometry, as they used it to solve astronomical and geographical problems. This enabled them to make highly sophisticated astronomical predictions that resulted in a greater and more accurate reckoning than previous civilizations, which nonetheless, had highly complex systems of measuring time and the movements of celestial phenomena.

To summarize, a consensus exists among all Muslims that the basis of our religious calendar is lunar, that it is determined by the crescent moons in compliance with the Qur'anic verse, and that intercalation to maintain consistent years is prohibited.

CALENDARS IN PRE-ISLAMIC ARABIA

The calendar used by pre-Islamic Arabs was an intercalated lunar calendar, which enabled them to plan certain solar festivals and manipulate the beginning and end of the sacred months for fighting purposes. In an earlier period, the Arab calendar was intercalated lunisolar, which is why some of the names of the lunar months reflect the seasons to which they correspond. However, at the advent of the Prophet's message, the sacred months, which were initially from the Abrahamic teaching, had lost their specific assignment within revelation's specified time as a result of the intercalation by the Arabs. For this reason, in his farewell address, the Prophet ﷺ prohibited the insertion of days into the lunar calendar.

In his intriguing book of seasons and sky signs, the

seventh-century Islamic astronomer and scholar, Abū Isḥāq al-Ajdābī, notes that astronomers tended to determine the Arab months based upon the estimated time of separation after the conjunction of the sun and moon (*mufāraqah*). He states that the first month was Muḥarram, to which the astronomers assigned a duration of thirty days, and the next month, Ṣafar, had twenty-nine; they continued to alternate in that order through the remaining ten months, with the last month, Dhū al-Ḥijjah, having twenty-nine days. Every leap year, a thirtieth day was added to Dhū al-Ḥijjah in order to make up for the fraction of a day, which is approximately three-tenths of a day per month. Abū Isḥāq al-Ajdābī continues:

> This is what astronomers have noted with respect to computing the periods of the Arabian months. This is based on the method of calculating the point of separation after conjunction (*ḥisāb al-mufāraqah*).[7] However, Arabs did not adopt this method. They always depended in their civil life on the crescent moons. Whenever they sighted a new moon, with it, they placed the commencement of the month. They commenced the month from the first night in which the new moon had appeared. They called this night the "the month's forelock" (*ghurrat al-shahr*), on account of the new moon appearing in the beginning like a *ghurrah*, which is a blaze or white spot on the horse's face. According to the Arabs, the month does not come to an end till the new moon is visible a second time, and from then on, they place the commencement of a second month.... When Islam arrived, it affirmed this practice.[8]

The every-other-month method is primitive and was rejected as unscientific by the polymath and astronomer, Abū al-Rayḥān al-Bayrūnī, who both refuted and mocked it. It was, nonetheless, an easy way to determine the months and is also a self-correcting system. The pre-Islamic Arabs, who were aware of the lunation or synodic month, did not implement it as the basis for their calendars; rather, unlike the later Jewish practice of calculation, they chose to sight the crescent moon. While modernists might look askance at these early calendars, the truth is that observational astronomy, for all intents and purposes, has advanced little in the last few thousand years. In fact, more than two thousand years ago, the Greek astronomer and mathematician Hipparchus of Nicaea (d. 125 BC) determined the length of the average lunar month to be within one second of today's accepted value and gave accurate calculations of the inclination of the ecliptic and of the changes of the equinoxes.[9]

Moreover, many ancient cultures accurately predicted the conjunction of the sun and moon in the ecliptic nodes, which enabled them to accurately foretell eclipses. What many people today do not understand is that creating a calendar, whether lunar, solar, or lunisolar, requires a thorough knowledge of the motions of the stars and many cumulative, learned adjustments. The noted American scientist, Stephen Jay Gould (d. 2002), in conversation with the Italian philosopher and novelist Umberto Eco, had this to say:

> Why have calendars at all? In order to predict the regular patterns of nature. In an agricultural society you need a solar calendar to know when best to sow

> your crops. In a society that lives by fishing you need a lunar calendar to know the tides. *Yet it is impossible to establish a simple arithmetical relationship between the two that would bring them into harmony.*[10]

Thus, the Arabs, who used calculating, sighting, and intercalation with their calendar, required a level of computation that had some relative complexity, and the ability to do so existed among those pre-Islamic individuals who were directly responsible for keeping time, which, as Gould points out, is a function of any organized society. Indeed, "The calendar is thus a synthesis that draws on scientific knowledge, religious belief, and political will. It reveals the way that power, religion and science interact."[11]

THE JEWISH CALENDAR

The Jewish community is the most similar to the Muslim community in both theology and devotional practice, as indicated by the sound hadith, "You are most like the Children of Israel." It is, therefore, not surprising that the Jews also follow a lunar calendar for their religious holidays, which was originally a uniquely lunar calendar, as indicated by the Hebrew word, *ḥodesh,* which means "month," or "new moon." At a certain point in their religious history, however, they began to intercalate in order to align the transitionary lunar year with the stationary solar year. Each month is still based upon a lunation or synodic month, in which the Jews add a given number of days a year, and an extra month every few years in order to maintain the lunisolar congruence.

How, then, did the Jews originally determine their

lunar month? They had eyewitnesses sight the new moon and convey the information to the Sanhedrin (assembly of Jewish judges), according to the *Catholic Encyclopedia,* which explains further:

> The Hebrew months have always been lunar, and extended from one new moon to another. The beginning of the month with the appearance of the new moon was—as it is still—of great practical importance among the Hebrews, inasmuch as the first of every month was to be observed as New Moon's Day, and certain feasts were affixed to the 10th, 14th, or other days of the month. The earliest appearance of the new moon was long ascertained by direct observation, and authoritatively settled by a commission of the Sanhedrin, and the intelligence then made known to the Jews at large, first by means of fire-signals, and later on through special messengers. In the present day, and for many centuries, this very primitive manner of fixing the beginning of the month has given way to a systematic calculation of the latter's duration, and the Jewish calendar is now constructed on the basis of a mean lunation of 29 days, 12 hours, 44 minutes, and 3.5 seconds.[12]

For more than a thousand years, Jews followed a calendar based upon naked-eye observation of new moons. However, during the reign of the Roman Emperor Constantius II (337–361 CE), persecution of the colonized Jews intensified, preventing them from communicating news of a sighted moon to one another. It was Rabbi Hillel II (330–365 CE) who first introduced to Judaism a new calendar based upon calculation and not actual physical sighting of the moon, in order to facilitate the observance of holidays for the oppressed Jews. The calendar was introduced in 358. "Its computations were designed to simulate the practical constraints of the observed calendar (including postponements and intercalations) as closely as possible," according to the Active Bible Church of God,[13] which also contains the following statement:

> Suggestions have been made that the computations should be changed, or that observation should again be used. It is clear that adjustments need to be made to the computed calendar in order to keep it synchronized with the sun and moon. But there is no consensus as to how this should be done, and, in the modern world, this needs to be done years in advance. *Returning to observation is idyllic, but totally impractical. The modern world requires plans for religious observances to be made months, or even years, in advance.* Only a computed calendar permits this. It is clear that just as "the Sabbath was made for man," so also "the Calendar was made for man." It is a tool to help us worship God. And an essential feature of a tool is that it must be useful and practical.[14]

One can see from this the compromises the rabbis made. Arguably, the Jews' initial abandonment of eyewitness sighting was because of undue hardship at a specific period in their history; and the result of one of their great rabbis' own human efforts to serve his community. Having said that, according to the principles of Islamic law, when the hardship that allowed the facilitating dispensation (*rukhṣah*) in the first place is no longer present, the license is no longer valid, and the original ruling must be restored. The Jews never returned to their original tradition of following a purely lunar calendar determined by eyewitnesses; instead, they continue to determine the new moon by calculation. Our Prophet ﷺ clearly warned us not to follow the Jews and the Christians in their abandonment of their own prophetic practices, and to be especially vigilant about this. Lamentably, he also informed us that many Muslims would not heed this advice. Predetermining our lunar months through calculation is a fulfillment of his prediction.

The Prophet ﷺ said, "You will follow the [erroneous] ways of those before you handspan by handspan, arm's breadth by arm's breadth, to such a degree that if they went down a lizard's hole, you would also go down the hole."

His companions exclaimed in response, "The Jews and the Christians, O Messenger of God?"

"If not them, then who?" he replied.[15]

Going from sighting to calculation is essentially to follow the Jewish abandonment of their original tradition. The Prophet ﷺ also said, according to a sound hadith narrated by Imam al-Tirmidhī, "What happened to the Children of Israel will also happen to my community, step-by-step...."[16] No disrespect is intended toward the Jewish or Christian communities, but this matter of strict adherence to our respective prophetic practices is a crucial point of divergence in our three Abrahamic traditions. The Prophet ﷺ saw himself as a restorer of the true Abrahamic practices that had fallen into dereliction among the Jews and Christians of his time. Among these practices is following a purely lunar calendar for devotional purposes and the determination of its months by the physical appearance and sighting of the moon.

CALENDARS AFTER THE ADVENT OF ISLAM

The Prophet ﷺ commanded the Muslims to keep track of the crescent moons and to inform him of the sightings. If a new moon was sighted for the devotional months of Ramadan or Dhū al-Ḥijjah (the month in which hajj is performed), the news was announced to all. According to Imam al-Tirmidhī, upon seeing the crescent moon, the Prophet ﷺ would recite the prayer: "O God, cause this new moon to come upon us in safety and sound faith, security and submission." Then, addressing the moon, he would say, "My Lord and your Lord is Allah."

According to Abū Dāwūd, the Prophet ﷺ would also say to the new moon, "A crescent of goodness and guidance, a crescent of goodness and guidance, a crescent of goodness and guidance. I believe in the One who created you; I believe in the One who created you; I believe in the One who created you." Then he would say, "Praise be to the One who caused the previous month to depart and brought us this month."[17]

In 637 CE, sixteen years after the Hijrah of the Prophet ﷺ, the Caliph ʿUmar ؓ instituted the new Islamic year based upon the first of Muḥarram in the year that the Prophet ﷺ had migrated from Mecca to Medina. The first of Muḥarram 622 CE, which coincided with the sixteenth of July 622 CE, began year one of the Muslim era. We are now in the 1428th year since that momentous event occurred.

Ever since then, Muslim astronomers and mathematicians have maintained rigorous and effective calendars for their respective eras, developed accurate ephemeredes that detailed the phases of the moon, and even provided crescent visibility tables for different climes. The Seljuq minister, Nīzam al-Mulk (d. 1092 CE), desirous of instituting a more accurate working calendar, commissioned the notable polymath ʿUmar Khayyām (d. 1131 CE), known in the West for his *Rubaiyat*, to develop a calendar based on the solar year. Khayyām was able to calculate the duration of the solar year to within decimals of that established by contemporary calculations. The calendar that he produced has an astronomical basis that is "more accurate than the Gregorian calendar with a discrepancy, it is said, of only one day in 3770 years." Unfortunately, his calendar was never adopted to replace the less effective solar calendars still in use.[18] Clearly, Muslims in premodern times possessed the intricate and detailed knowledge necessary to construct both lunar and solar calendars in order to organize their worldly and religious affairs.

Until very recently, the most widely used solar calendar in the Muslim world was the Coptic calendar. In the eighteenth century, the Ottomans adopted the Julian calendar as their solar calendar while continuing to use the lunar calendar for their devotional practices, basing it upon physical sighting of the new moons.[19] Shortly after the collapse of the Ottoman Empire, non-Muslim colonialists ran the administrations of much of the Muslim world; this led to the Muslim adoption of the current Gregorian calendar. Despite the almost universal hegemony of the Western calendar, Morocco, the United Arab Emirates, Egypt, Turkey, and Saudi Arabia still produce qualified sacred timekeepers who have studied the traditional science of horology and are capable of maintaining lunar calendars based upon both separation (*mufāraqah*), as is currently practiced in Saudi Arabia, and moon sighting, as is practiced in Morocco. My teacher and friend, Shaykh ʿAbd al-Ḥayy al-ʿUmrāwī, who inherited the position of timekeeper from his father and who still holds the key to the timekeeper's tower in the Jāmiᶜ al-Andalus in Fes, took me up into the tower and showed me the holes that had been precisely positioned to enable the timekeeper to simply look through them at the approximate outset of the corresponding points throughout the year where the new crescent would appear, if it were visible.

THE MEANING OF "CRESCENT" IN ARABIC

In determining the crescent moon, an important question arises: What exactly does "crescent" (*hilāl*) mean in the classical Arabic language? Furthermore, does our modern understanding of this word differ from the Arab understanding of the seventh century? The earliest and one of the most authoritative lexicons in the Islamic tradition is that of the linguist, al-Khalīl b. Aḥmad of Oman. His book, *al-ᶜAyn*, is the first scientific lexicon in human history. In it, he defines "crescent" as, "The first light of the moon, when people actually see the crescent at the outset of a month.... It is said, 'The crescent was seen' (*uhilla l-hilāl*) and not 'The crescent appeared' (*halla l-hilāl*)."[20] While other philologists permitted the use of the active *halla* to mean it appeared, he considered the passive use of the verb to be correct. In both cases, i.e., "It appeared" (*halla*) or "It was seen" (*uhilla*), humans are necessary to confirm the crescent moon, which means its birth is not an active event but involves witnessing. "The moon was born" (*uhilla*) literally means, "It was seen."[21] The exegete and linguist, Rāghib al-Iṣfahānī, explains:

> "Crescent" (*hilāl*) denotes, "the moon specifically on the first and second night"; after that, it is simply called "moon" (*qamar*).... "The crescent was born" (*ahalla*

> *al-hilāl*) means, "It was seen" (*ru'iya*).... "Birth" (*ihlāl*) can also refer to the cry one makes upon sighting the crescent, which was later used metaphorically to refer to a baby's cry upon being born (*ihlāl al-ṣaby*).[22]

In his *Lisān al-ʿArab*, Ibn Manẓūr says that the *hilāl* got its name from the cry of joy that those who saw it uttered upon seeing it. Furthermore, he says that the phrase, "the crescent was born" (*halla l-hilāl*) means "it appeared" (*ẓahara*). He also states that the crescent is "the new moon when people see it" (*yuhilluhu n-nās*).... According to him, "*ahalla r-rajul*" means "He looked at the new moon."[23] One of the great Turkish exegetes, Imam al-Brusūwī, says: "*Hilāl* (crescent) is the initial light of the moon that *appears to you* up until three days."[24]

Clearly, the crescent moon is something that is *seen.* It is a physical phenomenon, upon seeing which people tend "to cry for joy." Indeed, according to the American lexicographer Noah Webster, whose landmark dictionary of 1828 set a new standard for American scholarship and is the eponym for all Webster dictionaries, the English word "hallelujah" comes from the Hebrew meaning "to praise God" and the Arabic, *halla*, which means "to appear; to begin to shine, as the new moon; to exclaim; to exult; to sing; to rejoice; to praise or worship God." Webster also surmises that it is related to the English word "howl."[25] Of note is our idiom, "howling at the moon"!

THE ISLAMIC RULING ON CALCULATION

The foundation of any legal ruling in Islam is the Qur'an and the verified Sunnah of the Prophet ﷺ. All of the Qur'an and the Sunnah fall into four juristic categories:

1) Evidence that is decisive in its authentic transmission and unequivocal in its meaning;

2) Evidence that is decisive in its authenticity but equivocal in its meaning;

3) Evidence that is of probable authenticity but unequivocal in its meaning; and

4) Evidence that is of probable authenticity and equivocal in its meaning.

Ijtihād is not permissible in the first category. For instance, the texts that prescribe fasting are both authentic and unequivocal; therefore, no one can make a new ruling based on *ijtihād* concerning the obligation of fasting and its time. However, many texts, such as the majority of hadith, are either probable (*ẓanniyyat al-wurūd*) in the authenticity of their narrations or equivocal in their meanings (*ẓanniyyat al-dilālah*); this accounts for the differences of opinions among the qualified and authoritative imams in many of their legal rulings.

In the absence of decisively authentic and unequivocal texts, scholars may then and only then resort to *ijtihād*. For instance, the Qur'an states that a divorcing woman is to wait three menstrual cycles before the divorce is finalized. However, the Arabic word used is *qur'*, which can mean the time between her cycles or the time of her actual cycles. There is no known hadith in which the Prophet ﷺ clarified to which of the two the verse refers. This forced scholars to perform *ijtihād*, and they arrived at two different conclusions, both of which are accepted as valid. *Ijtihād* is therefore employed only in the absence of a clear and authentic text and cannot be done otherwise.

The second important rule to note about independent

reasoning is that any *ijtihād* concerning ambiguous texts must be in conformity with verified Arabic connotations as understood by the Arabs during the Prophet's lifetime and recorded in the accepted lexicons of the masters of Arabic lexicology. Hence, a thorough knowledge of classical Arabic (as understood by the first generation of Muslims) and other sciences is required before one can perform *ijtihād*. The Mauritanian jurist, Shaykh Muḥammad al-Amīn, says the following about *ijtihād*:

> It is a condition that anyone performing *ijtihād* must know grammar, morphology, and what is necessary from the rational sciences, such as the definitions, descriptions, and how arguments are set up. Furthermore, he must know philology so that he is able to understand the Arab usage of a word, as well as its common and legal usage. He must also know juristic methodology (*uṣūl*) as well as the science of rhetoric (*balāghah*).
>
> If an objection is raised against this latter condition—that the one undertaking *ijtihād* have this prerequisite knowledge—arguing that it is unreasonable since the great men of the past who performed *ijtihād* were prodigious and expert legal masters of reasoning before *uṣūl* was even codified, then our response is that the principles of *uṣūl* were inherent in their understanding and known to them even though the principles had not yet been systematically codified, as in the case also of grammar and morphology.[26]

If we understand these foundational principles, we can now look profitably at the differences that arose about how we determine the onset of the two months of Ramadan and

Dhū al-Ḥijjah, in particular, and the other lunar months in general. The Qur'an says, *They ask you about the crescent moons; say they are a means to measure your specific times and are also for the commencement of the hajj* (2:189). This text is decisive in its authenticity, because the entire Qur'an is decisively authentic (*qāṭʿī al-wurūd*), and it is decisive in its meaning, because there is no ambiguity about what crescents (*ahillah*) mean in the Arabic language, or about what the means to measure specific times (*mawāqīt*) denote; hence, *ijtihād* is not an option.

The Qur'an commands us to use the crescent moons as a means for determining our lunar months and our sacred obligations of fasting in Ramadan and performing hajj in Dhū al-Ḥijjah. An important point to note about this verse is that it specifies hajj and leaves Ramadan to be understood in the general meaning of the verse. According to the great commentators, hajj was mentioned in preparation for the final prohibition on determining the hajj based upon intercalation and not sighting, as the pre-Islamic Arabs sometimes predetermined hajj so they did not need to look for the moon during the hajj season. The magisterial Spanish exegete, Imam al-Qurṭubī comments:

> Hajj is specifically mentioned in this verse [as opposed to Ramadan] because it is among the devotional months; the knowledge of its commencement is essential, and [determining it using] intercalation is not permissible, as doing so displaces it from its proper time. *This is in opposition to what the Arabs considered acceptable at the time, as their practice was to perform hajj based upon calculation* (ʿadad)[27] *and alteration of the months. Thus, God nullified their words and deeds.*[28]

Another Qur'anic verse commands Muslims to fast for the month of Ramadan, unambiguously the lunar month known to the Arabs at that time. The verse says, *The month of Ramadan is the one in which the Qur'an was revealed as a guidance for humanity and clarifications of that guidance and a standard. So whoever witnesses (*shahida*) the month among you, let him fast* (2:185). Qadi Abū Bakr b. al-ʿArabī comments on this verse:

> "Month" here actually refers to the crescent moon of the month and was called "the month" (*al-shahr*) due to everyone knowing of its arrival (*li shuhratih*). Hence, God has obliged us to fast upon the sighting of the crescent moon (*ʿinda ru'yatih*). The Prophet's words [also add clarity]: "Fast upon sighting the crescent moon, and end the fast upon its sighting. And should it be obscured, then complete thirty days of Shaʿbān." Thus, he obliged us to complete thirty days of Shaʿbān should the crescent moon be hidden, and thirty days of Ramadan should Shawwāl's crescent be hidden. This is in order that we enter our [time-dependent] acts of worship with certainty and end them with certainty. Another hadith is even more elucidating: "Do not fast until you see the crescent moon, and do not break the fast until you see it."[29]
>
> Imam al-Tirmidhī relates on Abū Hurayrah's authority that the Prophet ﷺ said, "Note the day that the crescent moon of Shaʿbān [appears] in order to determine Ramadan's crescent." The next point is God's word in the verse, *So whoever witnesses the month, let him fast* (2:185). This is normally understood to mean, "see it with one's eyes"—in other words, sighting the cres-

> cent moon. This is reiterated in the Prophet's words, "Fast upon seeing it, and break the fast upon seeing it." *However, some of the early scholars stumbled on this issue and claimed that one can depend upon calculation to determine the moon's phases, as calculations could determine if the moon would indeed be seen if the sky were clear; they based this claim upon the Prophet's statement, "And if the crescent moon is obscured, then determine it (faqdurū lah).* But the actual meaning among the scholars of consummate expertise is "complete its number." This is why the Prophet ﷺ said in [another narration], "complete the number of days of Shaʿbān, thirty days." Furthermore, in yet another narration, he said, regarding the new crescent moon of the month after Ramadan, "If it be obscured, then complete a fast of thirty, and then break your fast"; this is related by al-Bukhārī and Muslim. Some slipped further by claiming that Imam al-Shāfiʿī said one could depend upon calculating, and this is a fall one cannot arise from.[30]

The Spanish master of the sciences of Islam, Ibn ʿAbd al-Barr, says this about the same verse:

> God says, *Whoever witnesses the month, let him fast* (2:185). He means, and God knows best, "Whoever among you knows, with a knowledge that is certain, that the month has indeed begun must fast it." And knowledge that is certain is [based on] either a clear and widespread sound sighting or the completion of thirty days of the previous month. The shariah also allows the testimony of two just witnesses who saw the moon on the thirtieth night [of Shaʿbān]. That is

> also sound, and therefore the previous month was of twenty-nine days. Some consider this sound only if the sky was clear and [the crescent not sighted], which is the meaning of "if not, then determine it (*faqdurū lah*)" among the majority of scholars.... According to Ibn Sīrīn, some of the great scholars among the second generation (*tābiʿīn*) understood it to imply a consideration of astronomy, the mansions of the moon phases, and mathematical calculation. Ibn Sīrīn said about this position, "It would have been better had they not done so." It is believed he was referring to Muṭarrif b. ʿAbd Allāh b. al-Shikhīr, and God knows best.

Muṭarrif was among the great pious and patient second generation scholars of Basra. Ibn Surayj also relates that Imam al-Shāfiʿī said, "Whoever is schooled in the ability to determine the course of the stars and the mansions and phases of the moon, and it is clear to him from his knowledge that the crescent moon will appear on a given night, but then, it is obscured by clouds; then, in that case it is permissible for him to consider it time to fast and sleep with the intention [of fasting the next day], and he will be rewarded." However, what we have found authenticated in his own books is that he considered the month of Ramadan to be valid only by a widespread sighting or sound testimony or completion of thirty days of Shaʿbān. This is in fact the school of all of the scholars of the Hijaz, Iraq, Greater Syria, and the West. Among those who confer are Mālik, al-Shāfiʿī, al-Awzāʿī, Abū Ḥanīfah and his students, and all of the people of hadith, except for Aḥmad b. Ḥanbal and those who conferred with him.[31]

It is clear that none of these men held the opinion that

allowed calculation to mean bypassing the actual sighting; rather, they understood calculation to be permissible only if visibility was obscured by atmospheric conditions.

Another important reason for rejecting the interpretation of the hadith "and if it is obscured then calculate it" to mean use of scientific measurements is the other narration, "and if it [the new moon of Ramadan] is obscured, then complete thirty days of Shaʿbān." In *uṣūl*, this is known as *mubayyin* (clarifying), and the former narration is called *mujmal* (ambiguous). It is a well-known *uṣūlī* principle that if a hadith has one narration that is equivocal and another that is unequivocal, and both are of equal authenticity, then the unequivocal is the one used for legislative purposes. Ibn Rushd clarifies this matter:

> The difference of opinion about [the commencement of Ramadan] results from the ambiguity in the hadith, "Fast based upon its sighting and break your fast based upon it, and should it be obscured, then calculate it." But the majority of scholars took the other narration, which states, "Complete the number of thirty days." Some of them said the measurement (*taqdīr*) mentioned in the first hadith means the new month should be determined with the use of calculation, and others said it simply means that you should fast the next day, irrespective of what your calculations may lead you to conclude. The latter is the way of Ibn ʿUmar. But the majority went with the authentic narration of Ibn ʿAbbās, which states that the Prophet ﷺ said, "And if it [the new moon of Ramadan] should be obscured, then complete the thirty days of Shaʿbān." And, since the former is ambiguous (*mujmal*) and

> the latter clarifying (*mubayyin*), then it is an obligation (*wājib*) to interpret the ambiguous one in accordance with the one that clarifies. Furthermore, this methodology is one in which there is no difference of opinion among the scholars, especially given that the two narrations do not involve contradiction. Hence, the way in which the majority [of scholars] have understood it is the correct one. And God knows best.[32]

About this point, Qadi Abū Bakr b. al-ᶜArabī, says this in his commentary on the *Muwaṭṭa'*:

> God has obliged us to fast based upon the sighting of the crescent moon and added to that an injunction to note the commencement of Shawwāl's crescent. Also, here is an interesting juristic point: some of the scholars of the second generation said that if the crescent moon is obscured, one may use calculation. Thus, if an astronomer says, "Tonight, based upon the crescent's angle of elongation, it is normally possible to sight the crescent had it not been for atmospheric conditions," we can act according to his statement in our fasting and breaking of our fast based upon the Prophet's statement, "determine it." In other words, they argue that he meant, "Calculate the position of the moon" based upon God's word, *We have fixed exactly the moon's phases* (36:39)....
>
> What a calamitous mistake they have made! I am not, of course, denying the foundation of the science of calculation nor of the discernable patterns of the mansions and moon phases. However, it is not possible that use of scientific calculations was intended in the

> meaning of the hadith for two reasons: Firstly, Imam Mālik discerned a principle in hadith interpretation which became a basis for those who came after him. Mālik said that the first hadith is equivocal, but the ambiguity in it was clarified in the second hadith, in which the Prophet ﷺ said, "Complete the number thirty." In other words, the second hadith clarifies what the first meant. As for the second reason, it is not permissible to rely on astronomers and mathematicians, not because their findings are not true but because people's beliefs must be protected from an association with celestial motions and future occurrences of conjunctions and separations. Indeed, that is a vast ocean should people be pulled into it. Moreover, there is a position, stated by people of understanding among the scholars of the second generation, that in the [specific hadith in which the Prophet ﷺ showed the number of days of Ramadan using his fingers], the Prophet ﷺ actually negated the use of the common numerals that mathematicians use. Therefore, it is even more likely that he would negate the use of celestial bodies and their orbits.[33]

What I find profoundly interesting is Qadi Abū Bakr's point that the Prophet ﷺ could very well have used the words "twenty-nine and thirty" when indicating the number of days possible in a lunar month. Had he done so, those he was speaking to would have understood him, as he was wont to state numbers on many other occasions as reported in sound hadith; he used high numbers, such as one million (*alfu alf*); he also used twenty-seven, twenty-five, and five; and he used the number ninety-nine in the sound hadith, "God has ninety-nine names, one hundred less one; whoever enumerates them will enter Paradise." However, he chose not to state any numbers when showing the number of days in a lunar month, as if to deter people from thinking about enumeration specifically when it comes to determining the lunar months. Hence, instead of saying the words "twenty-nine and thirty," the Prophet ﷺ actually used his blessed hands, showing with his fingers how many days are possible in the month, as if to emphasize using the most basic and fundamental human ability of sight. It is as though he were saying, "Look, see, perceive with your eyes the month, even upon my hands." This insistence upon *sighting* the moon illustrates so well "the sense in Islam that it is the immediate surrounding conditions, rather than any theoretical ones, that reflect the Divine will of God in its relation to men, and that it is these which should determine the sacred acts."[34]

SIGHTING THE CRESCENT MOON

The essence of the issue is sighting the crescent moon, which has been the standard practice of our community for fourteen hundred years with the singular exception of a period during the Fatimid reign of North Africa and Egypt. This is well illustrated throughout our books and the many examples given by our scholars. We should understand, however, that our scholars were capable of calculating the month or using astronomers to do so if they had seen it as acceptable. In other words, it was not lack of knowledge that prevented them but rather adherence to the Book of God and the path of His Prophet ﷺ.

The scholar and astronomer, Ibn al-Ajdābī states the following:

According to the Arabs, the month does not come to an end till the new moon is sighted a second time, and, from then, they place the commencement of a second month. A poet said, "Whenever I pass forth from the month [i.e., I bring it to a close], I enter upon [the period of the new moon of a similar month]. / It is sufficient for me to pull from myself the months and to enter upon new moons." One may say, "*salakhtu sh-shahr*," i.e., "I passed forth from the month"; in other words, "I brought the month to a close when I came out of it." One may say, "*wa nsalakha sh-shahr*" i.e., "and the month was pulled off"; in other words, "It came to an end." One may also say, "*ahlaltu l-hilāl*," i.e., "I entered upon the new moon"; in other words, "I sighted it." The Arabs followed this practice in computing their months. *At the dawn of Islam, this practice of observing dates by sighting the new moons was firmly established, and the obligations of fasting the month of Ramadan, celebrating the Eid al-Fitr, and performing the hajj ceremonies were dependent on this practice.* This is what they always relied upon and, by this method alone, calculated the dates....

When the month of Ramadan was once mentioned to him, the Messenger of Allah ﷺ said, "Do not fast until you sight the new moon, and do not forsake fasting until you are again able to sight it. If it happens to be obscured to you, count the days for its probable appearance." Another narration ends, "then complete the number thirty." This narration clarifies the meaning of the former. Furthermore, the calculations made by means of the separation of the moon after the conjunction might coincide with the physical sighting but

> also might not coincide with it; in fact, the calculation differs with the physical sighting more often than not. Hence, a calculated new moon will generally precede a sighted new moon by a day. It may also precede it by two days, but that is quite rare."[35]

The encyclopedic scholar and astronomer extraordinaire, Abū Rayḥān al-Bayrūnī, comments about this:

> The scholars of astronomy and anyone who ponders this [new moon's] situation extremely well concludes that the *sighting* of the new moon has no consistent pattern. This is due to the variations in the actual observed movement of the moon, which at times is fast and at others slow; sometimes it is nearer to the earth than other times; sometimes it heads north and other times south in its various ascensions and declensions through its ecliptic. Moreover, all of these various states occur throughout every point of the ecliptic. Sometimes its moonset is very fast at the points of elongation and other times it is slow. Not only that—these states also differ based upon the variance of longitude and latitude of the countries [from which one is viewing the moon], as well as the disparity in atmospheric conditions. Add to that the difference in people's eyesight and the gradations of strength and weakness thereof.[36]

It is worth noting that the early Muslims were masters of observational astronomy and far superior in their observations to modern astronomers, who do almost all of their work in theoretical abstractions and mathematics and are largely uninterested in actual physical observation of objects and events that are discernable to the naked eye, especially since the ancients have completed that work and there is little left to be explored. For this reason, many of the modern discoveries of observational astronomy have come from amateur "backyard" astronomers.

An example of the genius of Muslim observational astronomers is ʿAbd al-Raḥmān al-Ṣūfī, born in Iran in 376 AH/903 CE. His book on fixed stars is considered one of the three greatest works of observational astronomy. He is the first person to have observed the change of star colors, the change of star magnitude, the proper motion of stars, and the long period of variable stars. He discovered the Nebula Andromeda and also the Southern Constellations, which are attributed to modern astronomers in most Western books. He exposed many of Ptolemy's mistakes and faulty observations. Al-Ṣūfī's book was definitive until very recently and was quoted in modern astronomy books in the nineteenth century; it was the foundation of the work done by Stabius, Heinfogel, and Durer, which is the basis of all modern uranometry.[37]

Many modern Muslims, even those highly educated, believe there has been great advancement in observational astronomy. The telescope has undeniably enabled modern man to penetrate the heavens in unimaginable ways and to understand elliptical cycles of the moons and planets, as has the development of calculus. However, naked eye astronomy has changed very little. In fact, the reality remains that the observed motion of the sun, moon, planets, and stars is far less understood by the common man and by most astronomers than it was by premodern people who, in most areas of the earth, lived with the enchanting night sky much of the year; they navigated their journeys by the celestial phenomena and depended on such knowledge for the sustainability of their crops, harvests, and fishing. The Muslims in large numbers looked every month for the new moon and knew well where to look.

A wonderful account of the earlier Muslim community's interest in sighting the crescent of Ramadan is given by Titus Burkhardt, who witnessed its sighting in 1931 in the ancient Moroccan city of Fes:

> The keeper of time, *muwaqqit*, must also determine the beginning of each month, which begins with the appearance of the new crescent moon, and especially the beginning of the month of fasting, Ramadan.... On the evening that Ramadan begins, the keeper of time is not the only one on the lookout. On every rooftop people watch impatiently to see whether, following sunset, the young crescent moon will become visible. First one or two, then a quickly increasing number, espy the fine silver horn on the still light horizon. A cry of joy breaks out, for it was in this month that the Koran was revealed to the Prophet. This joy can be felt throughout the city.[38]

I have experienced and witnessed the same joy in my fellow Muslims who still adhere to this ancient ritual of moon sighting that profoundly connects us with the heavens and with God's power and wisdom.

This is not to say that theoretical astronomy is not also of great interest or that it has not advanced since the time of the great Muslim astronomers. On the contrary, building upon Greek and Muslim contributions, Copernicus, Brahe, and

Kepler revolutionized the way in which we now understand the heavens. Moreover, since the onset of the technological revolution, unparalleled advances have been made. Most of us, however, are like "the fool on the hill [who] sees the sun going down, while the eyes in his head see the world spinning round." In other words, we deny our existential experience of phenomena in favor of theories that, while true, deny our experience of the world. Notwithstanding all of the theories that tell us it is not the sun that is rising or setting but the earth that is spinning, we cannot exorcise our essential experience from our language. Even scientists will still speak of the sunrise and sunset!

Our English word "orientation" means, "a person's attitude or adjustment in relation to circumstances, especially political or psychological." In medical use, a person is of sound mind if oriented to time and place. The origin of the word "orientation" means "to know where the East is," which is something many modern people are incapable of; in other words, many are disoriented to place and certainly to natural time, as without clocks they are incapable of determining the time. The premodern peoples of the world were oriented to the sun, moon, and stars, and such phenomena connected them with the heavens on a daily basis. Sighting the new moon is a practice that maintains this connectedness, and this, in my opinion, is one of the legal rationales behind its injunction. But God knows best.

EARLY MUSLIMS AND MOON SIGHTING

To return to the meaning of *hilāl* in the Qur'an, it has been established that "crescent moon" in Arabic is a physically discernable object to the naked eye and that the Qur'an requires the crescents to be the basis of our months.

The questions arises: Did Muslims of the past differ on the subject of sighting the moon and its necessity in establishing the onset of Ramadan? The answer is they did not. Actually, they differed on two other points: the first was whether a sighting anywhere on the earth was a legal reason (*sabab*) for fasting in other places, and the second was on the question of what should be done if the new crescent is obscured at sunset on the thirtieth day from the onset of Shaʿbān. These were the only two points of contention. According to our great scholars of the past, a consensus existed about the commencement of the lunar month if visibility was possible. Let us now examine the proofs.

The current claim that previous scholars held that using calculation to determine the new moon irrespective of visibility is unfounded; calculation is a late innovation (*bidʿah*) that was instituted in Egypt for a short period under the Fatimid dynasty of General Jawhar in 359/969. Despite this forced attempt at calculations of the new month, it was rejected by the Muslim scholars of the time as an unacceptable innovation.[39] According to some historical accounts of the Fatimids in Libya, the Qadi of Barqa was put to death in 953 for observing the fast of Ramadan by sighting the new moon instead of following the astronomical calculations of the Imam.[40] What is particularly noteworthy about the Fatimid position is "their practice in using astronomical conjunction as the starting point for Ramadan was not, however, due to the complexity of calculating physical sighting, since that did not have to be calculated at all, it was enough to see it, but rather to their belief that their doctrines were scientific."[41] Other than the Fatimid innovation, there is no evidence that Muslims have ever advocated calculation in lieu of sighting until the twentieth century. This is a major problem today.

The problem appears to be twofold: the scholars who argue for calculation seem not to understand the limits of modern astronomy vis-à-vis actual sighting predictability, and the astronomers who argue for calculation appear to have little knowledge of jurisprudence. The earlier scholars, however, were masters of Islamic law and well-versed in both observational and theoretical astronomy; many of them were capable of producing highly accurate moon visibility charts. Today, the two groups tend not to communicate much with each other, and when they do, the jurists generally seem intimidated by the astronomers and fear appearing "backward" or ignorant in the eyes of modern scientists; meanwhile, the astronomers often look askance at committed religious people's adherence to premodern texts on issues such as moon sighting. Another serious problem that confronts all of us working in Islamic scholarly pursuits is that, lamentably, those of us engaged in the issue are simply not qualified to make *ijtihād* in the same way the giants of the past were.

SCHOLARS WHO PERMITTED CALCULATION

Only five major scholars are known to have allowed calculation as a means to determine the lunar month. However, if one examines what they said objectively, one cannot conclude from their words that they accepted the permissibility of using calculation in lieu of physical sighting. On the contrary, what they understood was that in the case of an obscured horizon, one could resort to calculation for the thirtieth day. Thus, they maintained that the Prophet ﷺ made obscurity a condition for calculation, and without the condition being fulfilled it was prohibited. It is important to examine the men and study their words, while keeping in mind that this opinion was rejected by the five imams and their schools, with the exception of a handful of scholars, whose opinions we shall also examine.

Three of these five scholars were from among the first three generations of Islam, the people whom the Prophet ﷺ referred to as the virtuous ones. The first and greatest was Muṭarrif b. ʿAbd Allāh, who was known as Ibn al-Shikhīr. What he actually said is, "If the *hilāl* is obscured [on the thirtieth day at sunset], then it can be reckoned with the mansions of the moon, i.e., which mansion it was in when it was obscured, or by way of calculation (*ḥisāb*)."[42] It is clear by his use of a conditional sentence "if/then," that he was not advocating calculation as a method in which we bypass sighting altogether. Rather, he was of the opinion that if after completing twenty-nine days of the previous month the sky was obscured by clouds or other atmospheric conditions, then it was permissible but not obligatory to resort to working out the new moon's birth, either through using the lunar mansions or some form of computation. The reason for his conclusion is the structure of the Arabic in the hadith that he derived his ruling from. When the Prophet ﷺ said, "And if it is obscured, then *(fa)* calculate it," he used a conditional sentence, i.e., *if* this happens, *then* do this. No one in the history of Islam, until now, has ever interpreted this hadith to mean that one could merely resort to calculation and abandon the clear skies of the thirtieth night. In other words, just as the operative cause (*ʿillah*) for the obligation of fasting during

Ramadan in the first place is the physical appearance of the crescent, similarly the operative cause for resorting to calculation is actually the obscurity of the horizon; and the principle that scholars demand for suspending rulings is that "rulings are contingent upon their operative causes in both their application and suspension" (*al-aḥkām tunāṭu bi ʿilaliha aw asbābiha wa tadūru maʿahā wujūdan wa ʿadaman*). According to our constitutional jurists, the "if/then" structure designates a rationale behind the ruling. So, even for those few scholars who permitted calculation, they recognized that the Prophet ﷺ had placed obscurity as an operative cause. If there was no obscurity, the ruling could not be applied, for the condition permitting it did not exist.[43]

One of Islam's greatest jurists, Ibn Rushd, known as the "Grandfather," clarified this last crucial and definitive point in the *Muqaddimāt.* If understood, there is no further discussion. He wrote:

> By consensus (*ijmāʿ*) of the scholars, it is not permitted for anyone who is determining either [to begin] fasting or to break the fast [of Ramadan] to do so by relying on calculation and relinquishing physical sighting. The only difference [of opinion] among the experts in this area is in regards to when the new moon is obscured by atmospheric conditions. Then, the question arises, "Can one use his knowledge of calculation or not?" Muṭarrif b. al-Shikhīr said, "He can do so privately." This is also the opinion of Imam al-Shāfiʿī [cited by Ibn Surayj], but what is well-known from his school is the position of the majority, which is that he cannot do so.[44]

Clearly, Muṭarrif was not advocating a sole reliance on calculation; he permitted it only if the crescent was obscured, since the scholars are in complete agreement that it is prohibited to rely on calculation in lieu of physical sighting. Their difference about calculation is perfectly stated by Ibn Rushd in the above remarks. Furthermore, another problem in relying on Muṭarrif as an authority to substantiate the position is that the actual narration from Muṭarrif was considered doubtful by the Spanish polymath, Ibn ʿAbd al-Barr, who was most noted for his knowledge of hadith and their chains: "This narration has no sound basis to definitively attribute it to Muṭarrif."[45] The second person among the first three generations known to have argued for using calculation—if the new moon is not visible—was Imam Ibn Surayj, and, as a student of Imam al-Shāfiʿī, there is no doubt that he was an imam of stature. However, he too is often cited as a proof for using calculation, without thorough explanation of his actual position being provided. Like Muṭarrif b. al-Shikhīr, Ibn Surayj did not say that Imam al-Shāfiʿī said using calculation was absolute; he also followed the hadith's stipulation that the new moon be obscured; only in that case did he allow it. Ibn Surayj's own attempt at reconciling the two hadith—the one that says, "complete thirty days," and the one that says, "If it [the Ramadan crescent] is obscured, then calculate it"—led him to conclude that they were intended for two different groups. Regarding the first hadith, Ibn Surayj maintained that it was meant for those who did not have the requisite expertise to calculate, so they were to complete thirty days. As for the hadith that ends with, "If it is obscured, then calculate it," Ibn Surayj believed it was directed to experts in mathematics or astronomy who are able to do so, and only to them.

This reconciliation of the differing narrations, however, was completely and utterly rejected by Qadi Abū Bakr, who maintained that the Prophet ﷺ would never provide two different codes for people. He wrote two long pages attacking the position, which many scholars have since commented on; this indicates the degree to which his emotions were aroused by the conclusion of a scholar as illustrious as Ibn Surayj. Qadi Abū Bakr wrote, in part:

> The hadith, "Fast when the crescent is sighted and break the fast when it is sighted," is explicitly unambiguous and a decisive text (*naṣṣ*) clearly meaning that one cannot bypass sighting the moon in either fasting or ending the fast. The reason is that [sighting] is the criterion given for the obligation and its determined length.... The Prophet ﷺ is telling us to bind your worship to physical sighting—to make your worship connected in its outset and its end with the appearance of the crescent.... Concerning the end of the hadith, "if the crescent is obscured," I have seen some of the Shāfiʿī scholars claim that to determine its birth, one can have recourse to the calculations of the astronomers.... This is a mistake that cannot be fixed, a slip from which there is no recovery, a distancing from which no nearness can come after, a humiliation that cannot find redemption. O Ibn Surayj! Where is your famous *Surayjiyyah*?[46] You follow this narrow rough path off the road. Tell me, what does Muḥammad ﷺ have to do with stars?[47]

The noble imam, who was also a proficient astronomer and considered astronomy to be a sound science, goes on for another page, but the above suffices to illustrate his antipathy toward the very idea of calculating the crescent moon's birth.

Finally, the only other major scholar from among the first three generations who is quoted on this topic is Ibn Quṭaybah. Ibn Ḥajar said in his commentary on al-Bukhārī's hadith collection, "Ibn Quṭaybah is not someone to rely upon in such matters,"[48] meaning that since he was a scholar of hadith and not a jurist, his opinion on the matter is negligible. Ibn Ḥajar goes on to explain that there were three interpretations of the hadith that ends "if it [the Ramadan crescent] is obscured, then calculate it":

> The first was the vast majority's opinion, which was that it meant to complete thirty days. The second was that it meant *consider the new moon ipso facto present behind the clouds* [irrespective of calculation], and fast as a precaution; this was the school of Ibn ʿUmar, and Aḥmad inclined toward that position. They also opined that should it prove to have been from Shaʿbān, then one must fast thirty-one days for Ramadan. Finally, "They said it meant calculate it based upon the mansions of the moon, i.e., what stars the moon had been in throughout the month and which were on the horizon at the time."[49]

Again, as can be clearly seen, the permissibility for calculation is only if the crescent is obscured. Despite that, all of the scholars who commented on the few that supported such a position clearly rejected it. What then would they have said about bypassing the sighting altogether, without the stipulation that the crescent be obscured?

Among the later scholars who have been quoted in support of calculation is the majestic and agreed upon Imam al-Subkī. He is, without question, an authority in *uṣūl.* Moreover, his opinion is highly regarded within and without his own Shafiʿī school. If one looks at what he actually said, one finds the same reasoning as all of the other scholars on this issue. Unfortunately, the point he makes is obfuscated by those today who advocate abandoning the Sunnah of sighting the crescent and replacing it with the "Sunnah" of calculating the crescent. Here is Imam al-Subkī's actual position:

> The Muslims are in consensus, as far as I know, that there is no legal consideration for the opinion of the astronomer that [the month begins] with the separation of the moon from the sun at conjunction if visibility is not possible due to the nearness of the crescent to the sun's [alignment], irrespective of whether this is before, after, or at the time of sunset. What scholars have disagreed upon is the situation when the angle of elongation is such that visibility is possible and can be ascertained by calculation but there were clouds that came between us and the crescent; [then, in that case, is it permissible to use calculation].[50]

This is the crux of the issue. If some feel, for whatever reasons, that they must break ranks with the five great imams and their schools, then at least let those who wish to calculate follow this minority opinion of a few of our great imams. People may determine the new moon visibility factor, and if astronomers say that it cannot be sighted, then they can reject the testimony of any who claim to have seen it; in fact, this is the position of many of our scholars of the past. On the thirtieth night, after completing twenty-nine days of Shaʿbān, if no one can see the moon anywhere on the earth, let them announce that since the astronomers have said visibility would have been possible had the atmospheric conditions not obscured our view, people can, based upon this weak opinion of a sound hadith, decide that they will fast the next day. However, there is no other sound position that involves calculation, and to bypass sighting altogether is to bypass an operative cause that God has placed upon humanity, and it cannot be suspended without permission from the Prophet ﷺ.

The last major scholar of the past who is cited as a proof for calculation is Ibn Daqīq al-ʿĀd. He, too, is an imam without argument. However, upon examining his position, one also finds he has the same reasoning as the others, and again it is either ignored or missed by those promoting calculation. In his commentary on *ʿUmdah al-aḥkām*, Ibn Daqīq al-ʿĀd explains his stance:

> My position is as follows: calculation is not permissible for fasting by determining the separation point of the conjunction of the sun and moon based upon the position of the astronomers who see the start of the new month as something that precedes the actual sighting [of the crescent] by a day or two. That is in fact innovating a legal cause (*sabab*)[51] that God has not legislated. But should the ability to calculate determine that the visibility curve of the crescent is such that it would be seen had something preventing its visibility not caused that, such as clouds, then, in such a case, the obligation to fast is necessary because the legal cause for the fast

> is there. The reason for this is that the actual physical sighting is not what is legally binding, given that it is agreed upon that if someone was confined in a cell and knew by calculation that the [month] had run its course or by attempting to understand the signs that the day was indeed from Ramadan, then it would be incumbent upon him to fast, even if he did not see the crescent, and no one informed him that it had been seen.[52]

Sadly, in the papers I examined that used this quote to support calculation, the first half of this quote was omitted, so that his actual position was entirely misrepresented. One paper stated that the imam did not consider sighting to be a condition, when what he is saying is that *physical sighting is not legally binding in the case of one who cannot see the moon*, which is why he uses as an example the man in the cell who has no access to sighting the moon nor to news of anyone who did. In such circumstances, the imam says one can resort to calculating or *ijtihād*. Upon reading truncated versions of the quote, one could perhaps conclude that the imam did not see visibility as a stipulatory legal cause before the thirtieth day. But in light of the entire quote, he clearly does, and would have had to because it is agreed upon and a clearly discernable fact in the Qur'anic verses and the hadith associated with the issue. In fact, while they are often used interchangeably, a legal cause is more general than a *ratio legis* (*ʿillah*). Imam Ibn Daqīq al-ʿĀd clearly argues here that to use calculation in lieu of sighting is *bypassing a legal cause that was legislated by God Himself!*

Another argument posited for calculation is that since we determine our prayer times using mathematics and predetermined schedules with great precision, why should we not calculate our months? While this point may appear sound, it is actually a false analogy because of the existence of a point of divergence (*qiyāsun maʿa wujūdi fāriq*). In the case of prayer times, the stipulatory cause (*sabab*) by which the prayer time is known is the movement of the sun. Imam al-Qarāfī devoted an entire section explaining this principle in his magisterial work, *The Divergences* (*al-Furūq*). In it, he states the following:

> Why is it that we can determine prayer times by calculation and the use of instruments, yet in the case of crescent moons for the determination of our Ramadans, it is not permissible to use [instruments and calculation] according to the accepted position? The difference is that God has stipulated in our devotional practice [of fasting] the sighting of the crescent moon and if that is not possible, then the completion of thirty days of Shaʿbān, and He did not stipulate the astronomical new moon. On the other hand, in the case of prayer times, He stipulated simply the entrance of the times and their self-determining times. Hence, we are able to determine them by any means possible. For instance, a prayer is conditional upon the occurrence of the sun's postmeridian phase. [With Ramadan] however, it was not linked with the conjunction's separation but with its physical sighting. And should the crescent be obscured, we complete thirty days.[53]

Imam al-Qarāfī was a scholar of astronomy and actually believed astronomy was decisive (*qaṭʿī*) in proof, which is why he allowed calculating prayer times unlike many other Mālikī scholars who did not.[54] He does, however, state conclusively that the sighting is a stipulation placed upon the community by God. In other words, the argument that it was only due to the innumeracy of the early community that people were told to determine the month by sighting and if, in the future, the innumeracy was removed, they could resort to calculation and bypass an attempt to sight the moon physically is an entirely modern innovation. It is clear that the imams are in agreement about the proofs that exist. Their differences occur only in relation to an obscured crescent moon that cannot be seen due to atmospheric conditions. In such cases, the position of calculation is still extremely weak, but, undeniably, it was upheld by some great scholars.

In rejecting calculation, our scholars were not denying the validity of astronomy. They understood it as a decisive and exact science used to predict the positions of the planets, stars, and moon. In fact, many of them were well versed in astronomy. Imam al-Qarāfī, who was a master of the mathematical and mechanical sciences, built a robot that, according to him, "could do everything but talk."

He unequivocally knew that the position of the moon was known with precision at any given time of the month:

> If a Muslim leader believes that the crescent was born based upon calculation, he is not followed, because of the consensus of the early scholars (*ijmāʿ al-salaf*) against that position. This is in spite of the fact that ability to calculate crescent moons, as well as solar and lunar eclipses, is discharged with certitude. Indeed, God has set a standard that the movement of the heavenly bodies and the orbit of the seven

> [visible] planets is on one system for all time by the determination of the Precious, Omnicient. God has said, *The sun and the moon are on fixed courses* (55:5). In other words, they are calculable, and that they will never change. This includes the four seasons; they too never change. And anything that is unalterable gives us certain knowledge.[55]

Similarly, Ibn al-ʿArabī describes in his autobiography that he had mastered many subjects at an early age:

> By the age of sixteen, I had read from the mathematical sciences, surveying, algebra, inheritance, the books of Euclid as well as what followed of trigonometry, plane and spherical, and I had studied the positions of the planets, sun, and moon and how to calculate them, and I had become proficient in the use of an astrolabe.[56]

Hence, when he says, "I do not deny the foundation of the science of calculation," he is speaking from theoretical and practical knowledge. Furthermore, the argument that the early community was unlettered, and once Muslims achieved literacy they could abandon the primitive practices of that period, is false and, in my estimation, degrading to that community.

Indeed, Ibn Ḥajar and others understood the hadith, "We are an unlettered community—we neither read nor calculate," to mean something entirely different. They did not interpret the Prophet's preface as an operative cause but rather as a descriptive statement, an important and necessary distinction in jurisprudence. Ibn Ḥajar provides the following explanation of the hadith:

> "Calculate," here, refers to astronomy and to the orbits of the planets because only a handful of them knew such things at that time. Thus the Prophet ﷺ has made the legal obligation of fasting contingent upon actual sighting in order to remove any burdens from his community, i.e., of having to struggle with computations of celestial orbits. This ruling continues even should later people be able to do that. Indeed, the apparent meaning of the hadith rejects any association of calculation with the legal ruling....Nowhere did he say, "If it is obscured then ask the people of calculation."[57]

Ibn Ḥajar recognizes that only a small number of people knew much about astronomy at the time, which is not dissimilar to our current situation, given the vast numbers of illiterate Muslims alive today. But there were, indeed, among the first generation of Muslims, some who knew how to calculate astronomical phenomena given that some were capable of producing an intercalated lunisolar calendar. Moreover, Ibn Ḥajar understood that the ruling was a permanent one and not contingent upon the innumeracy of his community, as some have said before falsely concluding that if people learned such things later, they could switch to determining their months by calculation. Even some well-known modern scholars seem to have missed this point. Ahmad Muhammad Shakir, whose arguments are used as proof for calculation today, said:

> The interpretation, "This ruling continues even should later people be able to do that," is wrong because the command to depend on sighting is explained in the hadith with an unequivocal legal rationale

(*ʿillah manṣūṣah*), which is that the community is "unlettered—we neither read nor calculate." And, it is known that a *ratio legis* (*ʿillah*)[58] exists alongside the ruling: if the first is present, the second is also present; and if the first is absent, the second is also absent (*al-ʿillatu tadūru maʿa l-maʿlūli wujūdan wa ʿadaman*). Thus, if the community removes itself from the state of innumeracy—that is, among them are those who can read and calculate; and the people are able as a group and individuals to arrive at certainty and a definitive judgment through calculation of the start of the month; and they can be certain of this calculation with the same certainty as actual sighting or with greater certainty; and they have removed the *ratio legis* of innumeracy—then they are obliged to have recourse to this substantiated certainty. They should then resort to establishing the crescent moons with only calculation and not resort to sighting the moon unless they do not have recourse to such knowledge, such as Bedouin people or villagers, who have not heard news from the scholars of calculation.[59]

There are several egregious mistakes in the above remarks that might lead people astray. The first mistake is that the shaykh uses one of the subtlest legal principles without any qualification. His statement that legal rationales and the rulings associated with them are inextricably bound, and that the latter is contingent upon the former in its application and suspension, while largely an accepted principle, is far from absolute in its application. In fact, the principle's application is much debated, as shown in its explication here by Ṣadiq al-Ghiryani:

> If the legal rationale is clearly defined [he means a *naṣṣ maᶜqūl*] by the Lawgiver,...or it is agreed upon by consensus, such as the prohibition of wine due to intoxication, and there is nothing in the matter that is devotional *(taᶜabbudī)*[he means *ghayr maᶜqūl*],[60] then in such cases the ruling is contingent upon the rationale and is suspended when the rationale is absent and applied when it is present. However, if it is devotional, then should the rationale be removed, the ruling nonetheless remains, as in the case of the Sunnah of jogging during circumambulation of the Kaaba...[even though its rationale, showing strength in the presence of the idolaters, no longer exists]. If the rationale is textually determinable or agreed upon by consensus, then the suspension of the ruling based upon the absence of the rationale is a point of *ijtihād*."[61]

The rationale put forward of innumeracy is not textually determinable, as many did not consider that to be the rationale, and it is certainly not agreed upon. Therefore, *ijtihād* in the matter does not apply.

Imam al-Ghazzālī and others have also explained that many rulings may have only one apparent *ratio legis*, but others are hidden from us, and, for that reason, "If the rationales are multiplied, then the ruling is not necessarily suspended, due to an absence of one of the rationales."[62] *If this principle is understood, then what follows should reveal the fallacy in such reasoning.* Few scholars understood the remark of the Prophet ﷺ to be an *ᶜillah* in the ruling; rather, they understood it to be a description of the nature of his legal system, namely that God does not demand specialized knowledge for anything that He makes binding upon all of His adult servants. Thus, in the hadith, the Prophet ﷺ describes his community, essentially explaining that we are an unlettered community by nature, and that his law is understandable in its general pronouncements to the simplest of people, so anyone can adhere to it.

Thus, sighting the moon is an uncomplicated method that God has provided for us to determine our devotional obligations, such as for fasting in Ramadan and performing the hajj in Dhū al-Ḥijjah. Imam al-Shāṭibī states the following about this principle in a chapter he entitled, "Principles Based upon the Unlettered Aspects of the Shariah":

> It is essential that in order to understand the shariah, we must follow the understanding of the Arabs upon whom the revelation descended in their tongue. Hence, since the Arabs used certain words to connote specific things, we cannot abandon their connotations. Furthermore, if [one contends] they had no common usage of certain words, then it would be impermissible to apply a meaning to the words that they did not have....
>
> The Prophet ﷺ did not ask of us computation of the sun and moon's courses in their respective ecliptics, because this was not common knowledge among the Arabs, nor was it from their sciences, and because of the precision demanded and the difficulties inherent in such a course of action. Rather, he has given us the preponderance of evidence in our rulings for the position of certainty. He has excused the ignorant, removed from them blame, and overlooked our mistakes; and this applies to many other aspects of

> matters in the [sacred law] in which we all participate. Thus, it is not permitted to abandon what the shariah has prescribed and go beyond this intended purpose; for, indeed, it is a dubious place and a slippery slope.[63]

Another crucial point that Shaykh Ahmad Muhammad Shakir made was that people are obliged to fast if they can arrive at the same certainty as, or at "a greater certainty" than, an actual sighting. First, what can give one "greater certainty" than actually seeing the crescent with one's own eyes? Perhaps what he meant was that modern science provides greater certainty than our own senses (sometimes true, but a dangerous premise). However, in the case of visibility of the crescent, it is simply not true. Perhaps this conclusion is based upon a lack of knowledge of modern astronomy. It appears that many modern scholars who have written advocating calculation are under the assumption that astronomers can now predict visibility with one hundred percent accuracy. While that may be true if they use as a criterion a conjunction separation of greater than twenty-four hours somewhere on the earth, it is not the case if it is less than twenty-four hours. It is simply unproven and thus not scientific. Only recently, due to unrelenting yearly inquiries by Muslims, has visibility prediction elicited some scientific interest at the British Royal Observatory in Greenwich and the U.S. Naval Observatory. In fact, on the Naval Observatory's website, the following is written in a section designed for Muslims:

> The visibility of the lunar crescent as a function of the Moon's "age"—the time counted from New Moon—is obviously of great importance to Muslims. The date

> and time of each New Moon can be computed exactly (see, for example, *Phases of the Moon* in "Data Services") but the time that the Moon first becomes visible after the New Moon depends on many factors and cannot be predicted with certainty. In the first two days after New Moon, the young crescent Moon appears very low in the western sky after sunset, and must be viewed through bright twilight. It sets shortly after sunset. The sighting of the lunar crescent within one day of New Moon is usually difficult. The crescent at this time is quite thin, has a low surface brightness, and can easily be lost in the twilight. Generally, the lunar crescent will become visible to suitably located, experienced observers with good sky conditions about one day after New Moon. However, the time that the crescent actually becomes visible varies quite a bit from one month to another. The record for an early sighting of a lunar crescent, with a telescope, is 12.1 hours after New Moon; for naked-eye sightings, the record is 15.5 hours from New Moon. These are exceptional observations, and crescent sightings this early in the lunar month should not be expected as the norm. For Islamic calendar purposes, the sighting must be made with the unaided eye.[64]

Many regard this source as representing the most advanced level of scientific knowledge on our planet, and yet its own scientists admit they cannot predict with any certainty that the crescent will be sighted on the first day of its astronomical birth anywhere on the planet with a naked eye. Most new moons cannot be seen before they are twenty hours old. After countless nights observing and following the crescents month after month, year after year, in the service of Islam, using highly sophisticated instruments to determine exact degrees of elongation based upon countless eyewitness observations, our premodern Muslim astronomers concluded that the crescent moon must be at least twelve degrees above the horizon after sunset, which allows for a setting time on average of almost fifty minutes. This is the visibility criterion that our traditional masters of astronomy provided on accurate visibility arcs produced in the periods of Muslim renaissance.

George Saliba, a leading expert on Islamic astronomy, says, "Although there was a religious prohibition on beginning the lunar month of fasting according to the computed time, a *zīj* text [computed astronomical tables] often included tables of lunar visibility to answer that problem specifically."[65] He also notes that Muslim scholars clearly distinguished betweens astrologers and astronomers[66] and that, after the thirteenth common era century, astronomers held public offices in all of the Muslim states. Their offices determined prayer times, and lunar and solar eclipses, and produced lunar visibility charts that helped people know when the new moon would most likely appear and where best to look for it.

Saliba states, "As a consequence, all problems that had any religious bearing were incorporated into mathematical astronomy and treated in those texts irrespective of the religious injunctions."[67] Thus, scholars of sacred astronomy predicted the birth and probable appearance of the new moons with great precision, regardless of the injunction against using those predictions to start the month. David King, the foremost authority on Islamic science, specifically astronomy, remarks that the Muslim astronomers predetermined lunar visibility by calculating the "difference in setting times over the local horizon. If the latter was forty-eight minutes or more, the crescent would be seen; if it was less, the crescent would not be seen. Using this condition and computing specifically for the latitude of Baghdad, the astronomer al-Khawarizmi, in the early ninth century, compiled a table showing the minimum distances between the sun and moon (measured on the ecliptic) to ensure crescent visibility throughout the year." [68] King continues:

> During the following centuries Muslim astronomers not only derived far more complicated conditions for the visibility determination but also compiled highly sophisticated tables to facilitate their computations. Some of the leading Muslim astronomers proposed conditions involving three different quantities, such as the apparent angular separation of the sun and moon, the difference in their setting times over the local horizon, and the apparent lunar velocity. Annual ephemeredes or almanacs gave information about the possibility of sighting at the beginning of each month. In brief, the achievements of the Muslim astronomers in this area were impressive.[69]

From this, it should be quite clear that the Muslim scholars were not backward or scientifically challenged, unable to understand that determining probable moon visibility was an exact science, even in their day, as many of them acknowledged. On the contrary, the great ones who wrote on the subject understood both the science of the problem and the entailing juristic considerations far better than any of us writing on the subject today. About that, I have no doubt. They were scholars of the highest caliber, and we do them a great disservice to believe that they did not calculate because "they had not yet distinguished between astronomy and astrology," or that they were incapable of calculating the moon's birth with any accuracy.

THE FIVE SCHOOLS ON MOON SIGHTING

While many modern Muslims have abandoned following any particular school of law, the overwhelming majority still do so at least nominally. In the United States, the Ḥanafī and Jaʿfarī schools are widespread, with many people adhering to the other canonical schools as well. This section will simply summarize the positions of the five schools of jurisprudence that al-Azhar University in Egypt recognizes as valid.

In the excellent text, *Encyclopedia of Islamic Jurisprudence,* produced by Kuwait's Ministry of Religious Affairs, the following opinions are presented:

> The relied upon opinion of the Ḥanafī school is that sighting the moon is a condition for the obligation of Ramadan and no consideration is given to the astronomers even if they were trustworthy. Moreover, whoever relies on their opinion has violated the sacred law (*khālafa al-sharʿ*)....Imam Mālik prohibited reliance upon calculation in ascertaining the crescent moon's birth and said, "Any imam who relies on calculation is neither to be imitated nor followed." Imam al-Bājī says, "If anyone did rely on calculation, I opine that he should not consider his fasting sound based upon calculation, and return to sighting or the completion of thirty days. If that results in him having to make up

any days, he should...."

As for the Shāfiʿī scholars, Imam al-Nawawī says, "Fasting is not an obligation unless the month has arrived. Furthermore, its commencement is ascertained through sighting the crescent. If, however, it is clouded over, then people are obliged to complete thirty days of Shaʿbān. They should then commence their fast irrespective of whether the next day is clear, or more or less cloudy. Thus, the means by which the month is determined are contained in either sighting or completing thirty days. There is no room for reliance upon calculation...."

The Ḥanbalīs do not depend on astronomical calculation, even if it was repeatedly proven to be accurate.[70]

In fact, this is the agreed upon position of the four schools, as recorded by al-Wazīr b. Hubayrah (d. 560 AH) in his book on the consensus of the four Sunni imams: "The four schools agreed that no consideration is given to knowledge of calculation and the lunar phases in order to determine the start of fasting, whether the people had knowledge of such things or did not; Ibn Surayj of the Shāfiʿī school dissented."[71]

Commenting on the legal text, *Sharāʾiʿ al-Islām*, the eleventh-century scholar Sayyid Muḥammad b. ʿAlī al-Musāwī al-ʿĀmilī explains the dominant position in the Jaʿfarī school on this matter. He says, "No consideration is given to predetermined schedules [for Ramadan]."[72] His usage of "predetermined schedules" refers to the calculation of the new moon based upon determining the elongation immediately after conjunction. He continues:

Undoubtedly, no consideration should be given to this

> method due to the multiply-transmitted narrations that establish that the months' onset is to be determined by one of two methods: either a physical sighting of the crescent *(ru'yah)*, or the completion of thirty days of the previous month. Indeed, had recourse to an astronomer been a proof, the scholars would have guided us to that position....The astronomers admit that its sighting (*ru'yatuh*) is only possible [and not certain], whereas the Lawgiver has made the rulings [that relate to fasting] contingent upon the actual sighting, and not the aforementioned arc of visibility].[73]

The shaykh goes on to remark that while there is a weak opinion that calculation may be used if the crescent is obscured, it is negligible.[74]

I think we can conclude from the above two sections that each of the schools, with the exception of the Ḥanbalī school, have weak positions supporting calculation, but none allow calculation in lieu of actual sighting; all of them stipulate that one can resort to calculation only if, on the thirtieth night, there is a cloud cover that obscures the crescent moon, and if astronomers have indicated that the moon would be visible. It was also shown that they stipulated that the arc of elongation after sunset must be at least twelve degrees, and that would mean at least forty-eight minutes would have passed before the crescent set. The current arc being used by ISNA's mathematicians is nine degrees,[75] which leaves less than a half hour before the crescent sets. Hence, the crescent moon would be, for all intents and purposes, impossible to see unless conditions were perfect and the time and coordinates of the particular spot placed it in an optimal position in relation to the sun;

even in that case, it would be extremely difficult to see with the naked eye.

MAGNIFIED CRESCENTS AND CONFUSION: SIGNS OF THE LAST DAYS

According to our Prophet ﷺ, one of the signs of the latter days is the magnification of crescent moons and people stating upon seeing a new moon that it is actually two days old. In a hadith related by Imam al-Ṭabarānī, the Prophet ﷺ said, "Among the signs of the End of Time is the swelling of the crescent moons (*intifākhu l-ahillah*)," and also that people will see a first-day crescent moon and remark, "It is clearly two days old!" The first sign is people's perceiving the crescent moons as inflated. Imam al-Ghumārī, the great Moroccan scholar of hadith said, "This hadith clearly refers to modern instruments....Indeed, the swelling of the crescents is not to be taken literally...but it explains how they will appear through a telescope."[76]

Imam al-Ghumārī believes the second part is related to the first. The second sign is that people see a new moon and think, due to its size, that it is two days old. In fact, I have heard this remark on countless occasions from Muslims who see a new moon; because it is over thirty hours old, which is when new moons are normally sighted, they think it is too big to be a newborn crescent and declare that it is at least two days old. This results from people's alienation from the natural order and the fact that few modern people ever observe the phases of the moon from birth to conjunction and rebirth. In a similarly extraordinary hadith, the Prophet ﷺ said, "Among the signs of the End of Time is that the crescent will be seen with the naked eye, and it will be said, 'This is two days old.'"[77] In another variant, the narration states, "Among the signs of the end is the hopping of the crescents *(intifāju l-ahillah).*" Imam al-Ghumārī's interpretation is that the news of the crescent will spread immediately throughout the world [since the word is taken from the hop of a rabbit: *intafāja l-arnab*, the rabbit hopped]. And God knows best.

Another problem that modern people face is that they rarely see the stars, in part because of light pollution. I have no doubt that if there were no electric lights at night in our cities, people would be far more inclined to think deeply about their purpose on this earth. People once followed moon phases throughout the world. Most modern people have never seen a crescent emerge out of the twilight before their naked eyes. On the few occasions that I have, I have been dumbstruck by the event and indeed "shouted for joy," (*Allāhū akbar*). Because people no longer see the crescent, they cannot understand how a first-day crescent can show up so high in the sky. However, some new moons are born over thirty hours after the conjunction and, depending on where it shows up on the earth and in the various time zones, it will indeed differ in size.

But our Prophet ﷺ did not leave us without guidance. Imam Muḥammad b. ʿAbd al-Rāziq writes:

> No consideration should be given to the relative size whether large or small or to the time in which the crescent sets. The *Ṣaḥīḥ* of Imam Muslim relates the following from Abū al-Bakhtarī, "A group of us had set out to perform ʿUmrah [just before Ramadan], and we alighted upon the valley of Nakhlah. We all saw the crescent moon [of Ramadan]. Some of us said, 'O, it is

> at least three days old,' and others said, 'No, it is only two days old.' When we arrived, we met Ibn ᶜAbbās and told him that we had seen the crescent. He asked, 'On which night did you see it?' We replied, 'On such and such a night.' To this, he responded, 'The Messenger of God ﷺ said, "God has extended the period [in which the crescent is seen] in order that it be seen (*Inna Allāha maddahu li l-ru'yah*)." It was, in fact, the first night in which you saw it.'"[78]

Imam Abū Bakr ﵀ says about the phenomenon of a larger crescent on the first day, "Our scholars have said that no consideration is given to either the crescent's largeness or its slimness. Indeed, it is related that ᶜUmar ﵁ said, 'Some new crescent moons are bigger than others, so if you see one after the meridian, consider it for the following night.'"[79] This year some people will invariably see the new crescent on its actual first night and exclaim, "O, that is at least two days old; so we started on the right day." And, if they do not see it until the second night, some will say, "O, that is three or four days old!" But that is not the issue. The point is that they did not start with certainty because neither they, nor anyone they know, saw it. It was calculated in someone's head and dispersed via the internet. The Prophet of God ﷺ spoke the truth.

Another important sign of the latter days is the general confusion that occurs in both religious and worldly matters. The Prophet ﷺ said, "In the latter days, people of composure will become bewildered and confused."[80] Unfortunately, because of a lack of adherence to the two things the Prophet ﷺ left for us—the Book (which states, "Whoever witnesses the month, let him fast") and the

Sunnah (which states, "Do not fast until you see it, and do not break your fast until you see it")—more confusion is added to the already existing confusion.

CONCLUSION

God has made the heavens one of His greatest signs. The Qur'an says, *Surely in the creation of the heavens and the earth, and the alternation of night and day, are signs for people of understanding* (3:190). He has hidden the unseen and the future from us and warned us: *It is God who has knowledge of the end of time, and who showers the rain, and who knows what is in the wombs. No soul knows what it will earn tomorrow, and no soul knows in what land it will die: but God is omniscient, completely aware* (31:34). Yes, there are discernable patterns in the world that are studied by the empirical sciences, but these sciences have limitations, and we should take care lest in our arrogance we think that we have control over our lives and the natural order:

> *Then when the earth takes on golden ornamentation* [lights of our cities seen from space], *and is all adorned, and people think they have power over it. Our order comes to it by night or by day; then we have it mown down, as if it had not flourished the day before. Thus do we explain the signs to people who reflect. And God calls to the abode of peace, and guides anyone at will to a straight path* (Qur'an 10:24—25).

God has hidden from us the power to predict the actual appearance of the crescent moon on the first day. Even modern scientists admit this. Yet, we wish to fit God's plans into our plans instead of fitting our plans into God's plans.

Convenience store Islam is the choice of the day, where we can buy a pre-packaged Islam that fits into our busy schedules. But Ramadan is God's month; it is a time of slowing down and reflecting, of looking at our lives and questioning ourselves, "Are we in harmony with God's creation? Are we bypassing signs right before our eyes?" God has veiled Ramadan's greatest night from us, and if He chooses to ask us to inconvenience ourselves just a little bit for His sake to seek out Ramadan's onset, then praise be to God. I find it altogether odd that a month that is meant to teach us patience and is called "the month of patience," is no longer patiently waited for by eager Muslims to see what God has in store for them tonight or perhaps tomorrow night. I believe sighting the moon is an intended purpose of Ramadan. It is indeed an act of worship, as the Prophet ﷺ has clearly said, "The best of God's servants are those who monitor the sun, crescents, and stars as a way of remembering God."[81] Every morning before dawn, the Prophet ﷺ would awaken, go out into the late night air, and look up in the heavens and recite the final verses of Āl ᶜImrān: *Surely in the creation of the heavens and the earth, and the alternation of the night and the day, are signs for people….*[82] The signs are indeed clear for those who reflect.

Ibn Taymiyyah wrote hundreds of years ago:

> It is impossible to determine, by means of mathematics, the exact time the crescent moon appears. For even though the astronomers may know that the light emanating from the moon is a reflection of the sun, and that when the two bodies meet in the conjunction, the light of the moon disappears, and when it separates from the sun, it regains its light, yet the best they can do is

> to determine exactly, through calculation, the distance between the moon and sun when the latter sets.... If we did assume that they managed to determine the moon's position at sunset, this would not prove that the crescent had actually been sighted. Visibility is a sensory matter and is affected by several factors, such as the clarity or density of the atmosphere, the high or low position of the celestial body, and finally, the strength or weakness of one's eyesight....When they realized that the shariah commands the sighting of the crescent moon, they desired to determine it by means of mathematics, and thus they went astray and led others astray. Those who argue that the crescent cannot be seen at twelve or ten degrees, etc., have erred, for one person can sight it at the smaller number of degrees while another cannot at the same degree. They have resorted neither to reason nor to revelation, and because of this, the eminent scholars in their field have rejected their views.[83]

What Imam Ibn Taymiyyah said is as valid today as it was when he wrote it. Several hundred years ago, a scholar in Libya was put to death because he refused to start Ramadan with the Fatimid ruler's decree of calculation. He spoke out against the innovation and lost his life for obeying God and disobeying man. Thank God we live in a time and place in which we can freely dissent if our conscience tells us we must. May that imam's death not be in vain.

Our Prophet ﷺ did not leave us without guidance, nor did our scholars leave us without elucidation of that guidance for they are the "inheritors of the prophets." In these latter days, the Sunnah is disappearing from the face of the earth. The Prophet ﷺ came to teach the simple and the sophisticated, the meek and the mighty, and he gave each his dignity and his place. In following his example, we follow the best in ourselves, and in leaving his guidance, we open ourselves to great calamities and tribulations. Allah, the Exalted, said, *So let those who oppose his command beware lest a trial befall them or a painful chastisement* (24:63). The Prophet ﷺ has commanded us in a hadith that is of no less authority than the Qur'an itself: "Fast upon *seeing* the crescent, and break your fast upon *seeing* it; *and if it be obscured, then calculate it.*" The meaning is clear, as has been clarified by the illustrious imams quoted in the preceding pages. They are my proof; after God and then His messenger, I have no others. What is left is to follow their guidance. And may God give us the success to do so. And Allah knows best.

NOTES

1 ʿAbd al-Ḥayy al-Kattānī, *Tarātīb al-idāriyyah* (Beirut: Dār al-Kitāb al-ʿArabi, n.d.), 1:77–81.

2 Abū Bakr al-Khaṭīb al-Baghdādī, *Risālah fī ʿilm al-nujūm* (Beirut: Dār al-Kutub al-ʿIlmiyyah, 2004), 22–24. (Note: The first hadith has a break in the chain and is considered *mursal* but is strengthened by other similar narrations according to the scholars. The second hadith is sound according to al-Ḥākim and al-Dhahabī. Both hadith refer to the muezzins who traditionally were timekeepers also. The Prophet's muezzins used to monitor the night stars to see how near dawn was.)

3 al-Nasafī, *Tafsīr al-Nasafī* (Beirut: Dār al-Nafā'is, 1996), 1–2:181.

4 Abū Bakr b. al-ʿArabī, *Aḥkām al-Qur'an* (Beirut: Dār al-Kutub al-ʿIlmiyyah, 1988), 1:140.

5 Abū Saʿūd, *Irshād al-ʿaql al-salīm ilā mazāyā al-Qur'ān al-karīm* (Beirut: Dār Iḥyā' al-Turāth al-ʿArabī, 1994), 203.

6 David Duncan, *The Calendar* (London: Fourth Estate, 1999), xvii.

7 This point must be underscored. It is clear proof that the pre-Islamic Arabs understood conjunction and elongation (*mufarāqah*). According to a hadith, the Prophet ﷺ states, "The month is twenty-nine days, so do not fast until you see the moon, and do not break it [your fast] until you see the moon." This hadith is miraculous because the month is never greater than 29.8 days. Separation will always occur somewhere

on the twenty-ninth day of the lunation, but it will not be seen until the thirtieth, if the hours remaining in the day are not enough to allow the crescent to emerge from the twilight on the thirtieth night then it will be seen definitely on the thirty-first night after the onset of the previous month unless it had been miscalculated, which can occur but will be self-correcting. This point is completely ignored in the arguments for calculation. In fact, some scholars considered the fact that the Prophet ﷺ said the month is twenty-nine days to be problematic, as it is either twenty-nine or thirty, which is how he described the month with his blessed fingers in the other well-known hadith. But the former hadith is also clear and is in congruence with modern science, as it is now known that lunation will never occur in more than 29.8 days, which is less than thirty days, just as the Prophet ﷺ stated! Moreover, the Caliph ʿUmar ؓ told people not to concern themselves with the relative size of the new moon. He informed them that some months it will be larger than others, which is consistent with modern knowledge because of the number of hours that transpire after conjunction. In a sound hadith in the chapter on fasting in Imam Muslim's collection, Ibn ʿAbbās told people that the Prophet ﷺ informed him that the reason God gave two days for the moon to be born was to insure that His servants actually saw it! Which is clear proof that sighting is an ʿ*illah,* or legal rationale as the particle of reason (*lam al-taʿlīl*) is used in the hadith.

8 Ibn al-Ajdābī, *The Book of Seasonal Periods and Sky Signs* (Islamabad: Pakistan Hijra Council, 1989), 34–35 (from the Arabic side). (Note: my own translation.)

9 Jan Gullberg, *Mathematics from the Birth of Numbers* (New York: W.W. Norton and Company, 1997), 462.

10 Jacqueline de Bourgoing, *The Calendar, History Lore and Legend* (n.p.: Discoveries Harry N. Abrams Publisher, n.d.).

(Note: emphasis mine.)

11 Ibid., 36.

12 *The Catholic Encyclopedia: An International Work of Reference on the Constitution, Doctrine, Discipline, and History of the Catholic Church*, ed. Charles G. Herbermann (New York: Robert Appleton Company, 1908), 3:166–7.

13 http://www.abcog.org/faqcal2.htm.

14 Nathan Bushwick, *Understanding the Jewish Calendar* (New York: Moznaim Publishing, 1989), http://www.abcog.org/calcomp.htm. (Note: emphasis mine.)

15 Abū ᶜAbd Allāh Muḥammad b. Ismāᶜīl al-Bukhārī, *Ṣaḥīḥ al-Bukhārī* (Beirut: al-Maktabah al-ᶜAṣriyyah, 2005), 612, no. 3456.

16 Muḥammad Ḥabīb Allāh al-Jakanī, *Zād al-Muslim fī mā ittafaq ᶜalayh al-Bukhārī wa Muslim* (Beirut: Dār al-Fikr, 1981), 1:382–4. (Note: The first hadith is agreed upon by al-Bukhārī and Muslim.)

17 Muḥyī al-Dīn al-Nawawī, *al-Adhkār* (Jeddah: Dār al-Minhāj, 2005), 318.

18 Cyril Glasse, *The Concise Encyclopedia of Islam* (San Francisco: Harper, 1989), 463.

19 Ibid., 96–7.

20 al-Khalīl b. Aḥmad al-Farāhīdī, *Kitāb al-ᶜayn* (Beirut: Dār Iḥyā' al-Turāth al-ᶜArabī, n.d.), 1017.

21 Ibid.

22 Rāghib al-Iṣfahānī, *al-Mufradāt* (Damascus: Dār al-Qalam, 1992), 843.

23 Ibn Manẓūr, *Lisān al-lisān tahdhīb al-lisān* (Beirut: Dār al-Kutub al-ᶜIlmiyyah, 1993), 2:693.

24 Ismāᶜīl Ḥaqqī al-Brusūwī, Abr. Muḥammad al-Ṣābūnī, *Tawī al-adhān min ṭafsīr rūḥ al-bayān* (Damascus: Dār al-Qalam, 1988), 1:148.

25 Noah Webster, *American Dictionary of the English Language* (New York: S. Converse, 1828). Note: No pagination in original edition; see entry under page-heading, "HAL."

26 Muḥammad al-Amīn b. Muḥammad Mukhtār, *Nathr al-wurūd ʿalā marāqī al-suʿūd* (Beirut: al-Maktabāt al-ʿAṣriyyah, 2004), 422.

27 *ʿAdad*: "what is numbered, counted, reckoned, or computed," from E. W. Lane, *Arabic-English Lexicon* (Cambridge: Islamic Texts Society, 1984), 2:1970.

28 Muḥammad al-Anṣārī al-Qurṭubī, *al-Jāmiʿ li aḥkām al-Qur'ān* (Beirut: Maktabat al-Bāz, 1993), 1–2:229.

29 This hadith is agreed upon by Imam al-Bukhārī and Imam Muslim. In fact, the hadith, "Fast upon sighting it, and break the fast upon sighting it, and should it be obscured, then complete thirty days of Shaʿbān," is considered multiply transmitted and has, by consensus, the authority of any verse in the Qur'an. See Muḥammad b. Jaʿfar al-Kattānī, *Naām al-mutanāthir min al-ḥadith al-mutawātir* (Egypt: Dār al-Kutub al-Salafiyyah, n.d.), 129.

30 Abū Bakr b. al-ʿArabī, *Aḥkām al-Qur'ān* (Beirut: Dār al-Kutub al-ʿIlmiyyah, 1988), 1:117–8.

31 Ibn ʿAbd al-Barr, *al-Istidhkār* (Cairo and Aleppo: *Dār al-Waghā*, 1993), 10:15–19. Aḥmad b. Ḥanbal's position is that of Ibn ʿUmar. Neither permitted calculating with mathematics but understood the "day of doubt," on which the Prophet ﷺ prohibited fasting, to be the 30th day of Shaʿbān, if the previous night was clear. If it was cloudy, however, Ibn ʿUmar and later Imam Aḥmad understood the command, "*faqdurū lah*," to mean, "consider it a month of twenty-nine days, and fast the following as a precaution." Ibn ʿUmar sometimes ended up fasting thirty-one days of Ramadan. Only a handful of scholars interpreted it this way. The majority considered it prohibited to fast on the

"day of doubt," based upon the hadith, "Whoever fasts on the 'day of doubt' has disobeyed Abū al-Qāsim [Muḥammad ﷺ]."

32 Abū al-Walīd Muḥammad b. Rushd, *Bidāyat al-mujtahid wa nihāyat al-muqtaṣid* (Beirut: Dār al-Kitāb al-ʿArabī, 2004), 227.

33 Abū Bakr b. al-ʿArabī, *Qabas* (Beirut: Dār Gharb al-Islāmī, 1992), 2:483–484.

34 Cyril Glasse, *The Concise Encyclopedia of Islam* (San Francisco: Harper, 1989), 96–97.

35 al-Ajdābī, *Book of Seasonal Periods.* (Note: my own translation.)

36 Ibid., 38. (See section entitled "Tafṣīl wa faḍl bayān fī al-āthār al-bāqiyah.")

37 See H. J. J. Winter's introduction to al-Ṣūfī, *Ṣuwar al-kawākib* (Beirut: Dār al-Āfāq al-Jadīdah, 1981).

38 Titus Burckhardt, *Fez: City of Islam* (Cambridge: Islamic Texts Society, 1992), 126.

39 Cyril Glasse, *The New Encyclopedia of Islam* (Walnut Creek, CA: Alta Mira Press, 2002), 97.

40 Michael Brett, "The Realm of the Imam: The Fatimids in the Tenth Century," *Bulletin of the School of Oriental and African Studies.* As quoted in Abdallahi Ahmed An-Na'im, *The Future of the Shari'ah: Secularism from an Islamic Perspective.* 437–438. http://www.law.emory.edu.

41 Glasse, *New Encyclopedia*, 97.

42 al-Musūʿat al-Fiqhiyyah, *Wizārat al-awqāf wa shuʿūn al-Islāmiyyah* (Kuwait: n.p., 1992), 22:12.

43 ʿAli Ḥasab Allāh, *Uṣūl al-tashriʿī* (Egypt: Dār al-Maʿārif, 1971), 145–149.

44 al-Hāj Muḥammad b. ʿAbd al-Wahāb al-Fāsī, *al-ʿAzb al-zillāl fi mabāḥith ru'ayāt al-hilāl* (Casablanca: Sharikāt al-Nashr, n.d.), 2:244.

45 Ibn Ḥajar al-ʿAsqalānī, *Fatḥ al-Bārī* (Beirut: Dār Iḥyā' al-Turāth al-ʿArabī, 1988), 5:97.

46 Ibn Surayj is famous in the Shāfiʿī school for solving an abstruse problem in a divorce situation, which is what the imam is referring to.

47 Abū Bakr b. al-ʿArabī, *ʿĀridat al-ahwadhī bi Sharḥ Ṣaḥīḥ al-Tirmidhī* (Cairo: Dār Umm al-Qurā, n.d.), 3–4:205–9.

48 Ibn Ḥajar, *Fatḥ al-Bārī*, 4:96.

49 Ibid.

50 al-Fāsī, *al-ʿAzb al-zillāl*, 1:20. (Note: emphasis mine.)

51 There are, in *uṣūl*, stipulatory rulings that entail something being made a legal reason (*sabab*), a condition (*sharṭ*), or a preventative (*māniʿ*) for something else. A legal reason (*sabab*) is that which when present necessitates a ruling, and when absent prevents it. In the case of sighting the new moon for fasting, it is considered a *sabab*, because the Prophet ﷺ said, "Do not fast unless you see the crescent, and do not break the fast unless you see it." What Ibn Daqīq is arguing is that if crescent visibility can be shown through calculation, which it can, and something prevents you from seeing it, such as clouds, then you can use calculation to determine the start of Ramadan. While this is a minority opinion, it is nonetheless a valid *ijtihād*. It does not, however, conform to the accepted positions of any of the four schools of thought, all of which stipulate the completion of thirty days from Shaʿbān, which is the soundest position and in accordance with the clear guidance of the Prophet ﷺ. And God knows best.

52 Aḥmad Muḥammad Shākir, *Awā'il al-shahr al-ʿarabiyyah* (Cairo: Maktabah Ibn Taymiyyah, 1987), 10.

53 Muḥammad al-Baqūrī, *Tartīb al-furūq* (Morocco: Maktabah al-Awqāf, 1994), 1:388–389.

54 My own teacher does not use them.

55 Shihāb al-Dīn al-Qarāfī, *al-Furūq* (Beirut: Maktabah al-ʿAṣriyyah, 2002), 2:177.

56 Abū Bakr b. al-ʿArabī, *Qānūn al-ṭawīl* (Beirut: Dār Gharb al-Islāmī, 1990), 73–74.

57 Ibn Ḥajar, *Fatḥ al-Bārī*, 4:102.

58 *Ratio legis*: Latin 1) the reason or purpose for passing a law; the problem or situation that makes a law necessary; and 2) basic principle or reasoning behind a law; the legal theory on which it is based. (Daniel Oran, *Oran's Dictionary of the Law*, 3rd ed. [Cincinnati, OH: West/Thomson Learning, 2000], 402.)

ʿIllah: Imam al-Ghazzālī defines the *ʿillah* as "a description (*waṣf*) the Lawgiver has added to the legal ruling as a cause for it and made it a sign of that ruling." Abū Ḥāmid al-Ghazzālī, *al-Mustaṣfā* (Beirut: Dār al-Arqām, n.d.), 2:463.

59 Aḥmad Muḥammad Shākir, *The Commencement of Arabic Months* (Cairo: Maktabah Ibn Taymiyyah, 1987), 15.

60 According to scholars of *uṣūl*, rulings are either rationale, i.e., the reason for them is articulated by the Lawgiver or easily discernable through discursive reasoning, or suprarational (*taʿabbudī*), i.e., the Lawgiver has hidden it from our understanding, and thus we trust there is a wisdom known only to the Lawgiver.

61 Ṣadiq al-Ghiryani, *Taṭbiqāt qawāʿid al-fiqh* (Dubai: Dār Iḥyā' al-Turāth, 2002), 28.

62 al-Ghazzālī, *al-Mustaṣfā*, 2:489.

63 Abū Isḥāq al-Shāṭibī, *al-Muwāfaqāt* (Beirut: al-Maktabah al-ʿAsriyyah, 2003), 2:58–66.

64 http://aa.usno.navy.mil/faq/docs/islamic.html

65 George Saliba, *A History of Arabic Astronomy* (New York: New York University Press, 1994), 78.

66 An important note—that some have ignored entirely in their attempt to argue that the main reason scholars rejected

calculation—is that astrologers were the people who calculated. That is false. Many Muslim astronomers were completely opposed to astrology and considered it prohibited by sacred law. Having said that, we must note that every astrologer was an astronomer but not every astronomer was an astrologer. Astrologers, even today, are dependent upon accurate charts of planet, sun, and moon positions in order to practice their craft. Isaac Newton, a redoubtable astronomer, was also an astrologer, as were Copernicus and Brahe!

67 Ibid., 79.

68 David A. King, *Astronomy in the Service of Islam* (England: Variorum, 1993), 248.

69 Ibid., 248.

70 al-Musūʿat al-Fiqhiyyah, *Wizārat al-awqāf*, 22:33–34.

71 Wazīr Yaḥyā b. Muḥammad b. Ḥubayrah, *al-Ijmāʿ ʿind a'immat ahl al-sunnah al-arbaʿah* (Riyadh: Maktabat al-ʿUbaykān, 2003), 77.

72 Sayyid Muḥammad b. ʿAlī al-Musāwī al-ʿĀmilī, *Madārik al-aḥkām* (Beirut: Mu'assasat Āl al-Bayt, 1990), 6:175–176.

73 Ibid.

74 Ibid.

75 This was confirmed by telephone with the gracious and learned Dr. Khalid Shaukat, who has worked many years tirelessly on this subject. May God reward him for his efforts.

76 Aḥmad b. al-Siddīq al-Ghuwārī, *al-Aḥādīth al-nabawiyyah li mā akhbara bihi Sayyid al-Bariyyah* (Damascus: Dār al-Albāb, 1999), 62–3. (Note: The hadith is in *al-Ṣaghīr*.)

77 Ibid, 62. The hadith is related by Dāraqutnī and al-Ṭabarānī in *al-Awṣāt*.

78 al-Ḥāj Muḥammad b. ʿAbd al-Wahhāb b. ʿAbd al-Rāziq al-Andalusī al-Fāsī, *al-ʿAdhbu al-zulāl fī mabāhith ru'yati al-hilāl* (Casablanca: Dār al-Nashr, 2002), 1:250.

79 al-ʿArabī, *Ahkām al-Qur'ān*, 1:141.

80 Abū ʿĪsa Muḥammad b. ʿĪsa al-Tirmidhī, *Jāmiʿ al-Tirmidhī* (Riyadh: Dār al-Salām, 1999), 548, no. 2405.

81 The hadith is related in Imam al-Ḥākim's *Mustradrik* and is sound. As quoted in Imam Aḥmad al-Khatīb al-Baghdādī, *ʿIlm al-nujūm* (n.p.: Dār al-Kutub al-ʿIlmiyyah, n.d.), 22–23.

82 Imam Muḥyi al-Dīn al-Nawawī, *al-Adhkār* (n.p.: Dār al-Minhāj, 2005), 67.

83 Jalāl al-Dīn al-Suyūṭī, *Jahd al-qarīhah fī tajrīd al-naṣīḥah mukhtaṣir al-radd ʿalā al- manṭiqiyyīn* (n.p.: Dār al-Naṣr li al-Ṭibāʿah, 1970). And Ibn Taymiyyah, trans. Wael B. Hallaq, *Ibn Taymiyya Against the Greek Logicians* (Oxford: Clarendon Press, 1993), 140–141. (Note: Some retranslating done.)